ADVANCE PR.

A STUDENT'S GUIDE TO CLINICAL SUPERVISION: YOU ARE NOT ALONE

Glenn Boyd has written a very appropriate and effective book on clinical supervision for mental health professionals who are beginning their professional training. He rightly emphasizes the importance of clinical supervision at this early stage of training and explains this importance to the student professional very clearly. They are entering a professional world that requires an exceptional ability to relate appropriately, openly and effectively to others, to be able to listen attentively and share honestly and to develop the critical and innovative thinking essential for mental health work. This can't be learned by just observing and reading professional texts. It must be learned relationally in interaction with others. Clinical supervision provides an excellent context for this to occur. Dr. Boyd's book, *A Student's Guide to Clinical Supervision: You Are Not Alone*, offers a wonderful opportunity for the professional in training to make the most of the clinical supervision that will be an integral part of his/her training. I was very impressed by his sensitivity to the professional world the graduate students are entering and his ability to write this book in a way that can be very understandable to the beginning student.

~ *Robert Cottor, M.D.*
Taos Institute Board of Directors

A Student's Guide to Clinical Supervision: You Are Not Alone is a ground-breaking book that speaks to the often forgotten person in supervision, the "supervisee". Written from Boyd's years of experience as a supervisor of mental health profession graduate students and new professionals in the field, this book is a must read for them and also for supervisors who want to be the best. It gives the reader a bonus: a glimpse of what makes Boyd such a well-respected and sought-after supervisor and what can be learned from his understanding and know-how of the supervision process.

~ *Harlene Anderson, PhD.*
Houston Galveston Institute
Taos Institute

A Student's Guide

TO CLINICAL SUPERVISION

YOU ARE NOT ALONE

Glenn E. Boyd

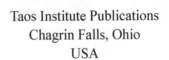

Taos Institute Publications
Chagrin Falls, Ohio
USA

A Student's Guide to Clinical Supervision
YOU ARE NOT ALONE

The Cover: The photo on the front cover of this book is in
the Orkneys, Scotland

Cover Photo: Glenn E. Boyd
Book Design: Debbi Stocco, mybookdesigner.com

Library of Congress Control Number: 2014938778

Taos Institute Publications
A Division of the Taos Institute
Chagrin Falls, Ohio
USA

ISBN 13: 978-1-938552-22-9
ISBN 10: 1-938552-22-9   PRINTED IN THE USA AND IN THE UK

Introduction to
Taos Institute Publications

The Taos Institute is a nonprofit organization dedicated to the development of social constructionist theory and practice for purposes of world benefit. Constructionist theory and practice locate the source of meaning, value, and action in communicative relations among people. Our major investment is in fostering relational processes that can enhance the welfare of people and the world in which they live. Taos Institute Publications offers contributions to cutting-edge theory and practice in social construction. Our books are designed for scholars, practitioners, students, and the openly curious public. **The Focus Book Series** provides brief introductions and overviews that illuminate theories, concepts, and useful practices. **The Tempo Book Series** is especially dedicated to the general public and to practitioners. **The Books for Professionals Series** provides in-depth works that focus on recent developments in theory and practice. **WorldShare Books** is an online offering of books in PDF format for free download from our website. Our books are particularly relevant to social scientists and to practitioners concerned with individual, family, organizational, community, and societal change.

—Kenneth J. Gergen
President, Board of Directors,
The Taos Institute

Taos Institute Board of Directors

For information about the Taos Institute and social constructionism visit:
www.taosinstitute.com

Taos Institute Publications

Focus Book Series

A Student's Guide to Clinical Supervision: You Are Not Alone, (2014) by Glenn E. Boyd

When Stories Clash: Addressing Conflict with Narrative Mediation, (2013) by Gerald Monk, and John Winslade

Bereavement Support Groups: Breathing Life into Stories of the Dead, (2012) by Lorraine Hedtke

The Appreciative Organization, Revised Edition (2008) by Harlene Anderson, David Cooperrider, Kenneth J. Gergen, Mary Gergen, Sheila McNamee, Jane Watkins, and Diana Whitney

Appreciative Inquiry: A Positive Approach to Building Cooperative Capacity, (2005) by Frank Barrett and Ronald Fry

Dynamic Relationships: Unleashing the Power of Appreciative Inquiry in Daily Living, (2005) by Jacqueline Stavros and Cheri B. Torres

Appreciative Sharing of Knowledge: Leveraging Knowledge Management for Strategic Change, (2004) by Tojo Thatchenkery

Social Construction: Entering the Dialogue, (2004) by Kenneth J. Gergen, and Mary Gergen

Appreciative Leaders: In the Eye of the Beholder, (2001) edited by Marge Schiller, Bea Mah Holland, and Deanna Riley

Experience AI: A Practitioner's Guide to Integrating Appreciative Inquiry and Experiential Learning, (2001) by Miriam Ricketts and Jim Willis

Taos Tempo Series:
Collaborative Practices for Changing Times

U&ME: Communicating in Moments that Matter, (2013) by John Stewart

Developing Relational Leadership: Resources for Developing Reflexive Organizational Practices, (2012) by Carsten Hornstrup, Jesper Loehr-Petersen, Joergen Gjengedal Madsen, Thomas Johansen, Allan Vinther Jensen

Practicing Relational Ethics in Organizations, (2012) by Gitte Haslebo and Maja Loua Haslebo

Healing Conversations Now: Enhance Relationships with Elders and Dying Loved Ones, (2011) by Joan Chadbourne and Tony Silbert

Riding the Current: How to Deal with the Daily Deluge of Data, (2010) by Madelyn Blair

Ordinary Life Therapy: Experiences from a Collaborative Systemic Practice, (2009) by Carina Håkansson

Mapping Dialogue: Essential Tools for Social Change, (2008) by Marianne "Mille" Bojer, Heiko Roehl, Mariane Knuth-Hollesen, and Colleen Magner

Positive Family Dynamics: Appreciative Inquiry Questions to Bring Out the Best in Families, (2008) by Dawn Cooperrider Dole, Jen Hetzel Silbert, Ada Jo Mann, and Diana Whitney

Books for Professionals Series

New Horizons in Buddhist Psychology: Relational Buddhism for Collaborative Practitioners, (2010) edited by Maurits G.T. Kwee

Positive Approaches to Peacebuilding: A Resource for Innovators, (2010) edited by Cynthia Sampson, Mohammed Abu-Nimer, Claudia Liebler, and Diana Whitney

Social Construction on the Edge: 'Withness'-Thinking & Embodiment, (2010) by John Shotter

Joined Imagination: Writing and Language in Therapy, (2009) by Peggy Penn

Celebrating the Other: A Dialogic Account of Human Nature, (reprint 2008) by Edward Sampson

Conversational Realities Revisited: Life, Language, Body and World, (2008) by John Shotter

Horizons in Buddhist Psychology: Practice, Research and Theory, (2006) edited by Maurits Kwee, Kenneth J. Gergen, and Fusako Koshikawa

Therapeutic Realities: Collaboration, Oppression and Relational Flow, (2005) by Kenneth J. Gergen

SocioDynamic Counselling: A Practical Guide to Meaning Making, (2004) by R. Vance Peavy

Experiential Exercises in Social Construction—A Fieldbook for Creating Change, (2004) by Robert Cottor, Alan Asher, Judith Levin, and Cindy Weiser

Dialogues About a New Psychology, (2004) by Jan Smedslund

For book information and ordering, visit Taos Institute Publications at:
www.taosinstitutepublications.net
For further information, call: 1-888-999-TAOS, 1-440-338-6733
Email: info@taosoinstitute.net

Table of Contents

CHAPTER 1

Introduction: Why Do You Need a Student's Guide to Clinical
Supervision?... 11

CHAPTER 2

What is Clinical Supervision and Why is it Important?............................ 21

CHAPTER 3

The Role of the Student in Successful Supervision.................................... 34

CHAPTER 4

The Role of the Supervisor in Successful Supervision............................. 50

CHAPTER 5

The Role of the Collaborative Learning Community in Successful
Supervision... 63

CHAPTER 6

The Role of the Client in Successful Supervision....................................... 78

CHAPTER 7

Competence: The Holy Grail in Successful Supervision 89

CHAPTER 8

Conclusion: Lessons from Graduation Day.. 101

References and Resources 107

CHAPTER 1

INTRODUCTION: WHY DO YOU NEED A STUDENT'S GUIDE TO CLINICAL SUPERVISION?

S ANDY AND GREG WOULD LIKE to welcome you to this orientation to their world. Sandy is an energetic and compassionate educator who for years has seen what family life can do to children, for good and ill. She grew up in a rough neighborhood, but had a lot of support from her family and church. Greg is a forty-two year old retired military veteran whose experience with combat trauma made him want to help other veterans recovering from Post-Traumatic Stress Disorder. These two graduate students are currently engaged in the kinds of experiences you will be having as you make your way through the training process to become a mental health professional. They count themselves lucky to be in a program that emphasizes the importance of collaborative learning, which gives them on-the-job training in the kind of relational sensitivity that makes for high-quality care. They also value the relationships they have with the faculty members and clinical supervisors.

Let me define some words right away. The word "clinical" refers to interaction with clients and patients. "Administrative supervision" refers to the management side of being a mental health professional, whether one is still training or already working. This book will focus on clinical supervision, which helps provide students with the knowledge of how to interact with clients and patients for their maximum benefit. Sandy and Greg hope that you will learn something from hearing about their experiences with supervision, whether your goal is to become a professional counselor, marriage and family therapist, social worker, psychologist, chemical dependency counselor, or any other type of helping person.

Even though Greg and Sandy are fictitious, they represent composites of all the students that I have taught and supervised. I have been there, too. A long time ago, I entered the internship phase of my training without a clue about how to take advantage of the rich potential of the opportunity. Many years later, after teaching and supervising beginning students, I began to realize that students might be better able to understand and integrate the myriad aspects and situations demanding attention in the training process if they have already been informed and encouraged about the rich opportunities available in the clinical supervision setting. My doctoral dissertation (Boyd, 2011) focused on how graduate school students experience the process of supervision and training. I learned that they were able to cope with what I termed the integration anxiety of the process by maximizing collaborative learning. What the students valued most was the safety and openness of both the learning environment and their supervisors.

If reading this introduction means you're either considering becoming a mental health professional or have already been accepted into a training program, the main thing to know is that you are not alone. I mean this in two senses. First, you will be joining a rapidly growing community of people like Greg and Sandy who see the tremendous need for competent, highly skilled professional helpers in today's society. Second, you will be accompanied in the training process by experienced professionals who will supervise the developing work of future colleagues like you. Every one of them has been through what you will go through.

This book will quickly bring you up to speed on how all of this works. It is true that becoming a mental health professional is a difficult and challenging journey. That's why you should consider it. This definitely won't be the last time I share with you one of my favorite quotes: "All excellent things are as difficult as they are rare," writes Baruch Spinoza. These words challenge us to realize that some difficult things are worth the trouble because people who do them well are rare. Don't say I didn't warn you when you think to yourself, "This is really difficult." Training to be a mental health professional will be a challenging but rewarding experience, and getting the most out of your training is necessary for future effectiveness.

If you dream of joining the community of people who want to do these things well, please consider working your way through this book at least as carefully as you are considering becoming a mental health professional. By the time you reach the last page, you will have a good orientation to most training programs anywhere in the world. Some things are the same no matter where you go.

When it comes to working with people who need specialized professional help for a difficult problem or a troubling condition, there is no substitute for the good old-fashioned apprenticeship model in which a more experienced mental health professional instructs, guides, models, and encourages the developing student. That more experienced person is usually a faculty person called a supervisor.

THE "SUPER" PART OF SUPERVISOR

You may be wondering about that word, "supervisor." In fact you may be asking yourself, "What's up with the 'super' part of the word 'supervisor?'" Good question. First, that person is not a super-hero like Superwoman or Superman. There is no Supervisor Person in colorful tights who sweeps down out of the clouds to rescue the confused rookie therapist in distress. We're not talking gods and goddesses here. Despite the fact that it is a little odd, the word describes not only a more experienced colleague, but also an essential relationship with someone who will probably like you and want to encourage you as you grow into a competent professional.

Second, taken literally the word refers not only to a person, but also to a process of "overseeing" or "seeing from above," in the sense of being responsible for the work of another. But a clinical supervisor is definitely not someone who "looks down" on you. Most supervisors see themselves not as standing above as much as standing alongside of a student therapist. As I said before, *you are not alone in this process.* The instant you decide to begin training to become a mental health professional, you will meet people who will help you get started. You may even meet the person who will eventually supervise your earliest attempts at practicing counseling skills. Don't worry. If you believe in the old saying, "When a student is ready to learn, a teacher will appear," you will probably find teachers and supervisors everywhere you turn.

THE STUDENT GETS TO BE SUPER, TOO

One distinctive feature of this book is the idea that students in a clinical training program should be well informed about supervision as early as possible. Traditionally, most students have learned about supervision only when they began working with a supervisor in the practicum phase of their training, which is when a student begins to work with clients in the presence of a supervisor. The student is almost always accompanied by a small group of peers that are in the same program. I will make the case throughout this book that clinical supervision is such an important part of a student's development as a mental health professional that training programs should provide information and orientation into the clinical supervision experience as early as possible.

A second distinctive suggestion that I make throughout this book is that you learn as soon as you can to engage the process of supervision *proactively and assertively,* without apology and without fear. Express yourself! Be an active, curious learner who asks questions about anything and everything! Make the most of the supervisor's experience. The supervisor will be a mentor and guide, just as I hope this book will be a guide for you as you consider how to approach your training program.

THE ULTIMATE STUDENT'S GUIDE TO SUPERVISION

We might start by reflecting on what a guide does in any situation. Not a guidebook, but a living, breathing person. If you went with a group to take photographs in a garden known for its rare flowering plants, what would you expect a guide to do? In the same way, what do you have a right to expect from the supervisors with whom you train? *Your supervisors are in fact the ultimate student's guide to supervision.* Not this book. The best guides are the people who will help you reach your goals. They are interested, even passionate about their area of expertise. They are well informed and welcoming to others eager to share their experience.

Good clinical supervisors make you glad that you decided to take on the arduous task of a training program. In addition to being guides, they are good teachers and good conversationalists. They like to answer questions, as opposed to the teacher who shames students for not already knowing the answer. In addition, they have a gift for encouraging and reassuring those who want to learn from them. A good guide hopes that you might value what he or she has learned to value.

A competent guide not only offers an experience, but also can articulate the experience by explaining its relevance to your growing understanding of how the whole system works. How would our photography guide know what might be relevant to the interests of those hoping to take photos of rare flowers? Obviously, guides must be good listeners who are able to determine what is relevant to the student and what is not. In other words, they will be open and understanding about what the student *wants* from the supervision experience, while at the same time guiding the student to gain the knowledge that he or she *needs* as a future mental health professional. In my opinion, a good guide has better-than-average social skills and is able to understand and relate to the personalities and needs of different students. These attributes will come in handy when you begin to work with real clients.

A guide accompanies fellow adventurers through unfamiliar terrain. The students know that they are not alone in the new experience. That safety enhances a student's motivation to absorb as much as possible from the experience. The guide may be a seasoned professional or have only a few years of experience, but she is more familiar with the territory than the novice adventurers who depend on that additional experience. Students get exposure to both the unfamiliar territory and the guide's experience. The guide interprets the student's experience by naming and explaining things, thus giving meaning to the student's observations. The student next learns to interpret his or her own experience. We cannot avoid making sense of things. It's what we do as human beings. By making sense of things, we plug the unfamiliar into the familiar, thereby expanding our working understanding of the new territory.

ARE YOU READY TO GET ON WITH IT?

If you have read this far, you're hopefully serious about getting as much out of your training experience as possible. That's what this book is all about, and I hope it will function as something of a guide as well. In the pages ahead, you will begin to get a sense of the various elements that define good clinical supervision. I will try to keep the dry academic stuff to a minimum, but some of it is actually interesting, as you will see. You may be surprised to see how complex and complicated supervision can be. In fact, you may have a new appreciation for the people who attempt to take on the role of supervisor.

You will hear more about the role of the student in successful supervision, as well as the role of the supervisor. As I said, you are not alone in this process. Other people play an important role in successful training: the collaborative learning community and the client. Those two get left out sometimes. Finally, I will introduce you to the important notion of competence and how it is revolutionizing both practice and training.

If you can embrace that idea that anything of lasting value takes time and effort, then you stand at the beginning of a transformative process that will change your life. Your personal courage and resilience will not only help you get through the hard parts, but they also will open doors into the kind of wisdom required to be able to help people professionally. Remember: You are not alone. As you learn how important that can be in your own professional development, you will be learning how important it can be for your future clients. You have already begun to invest in your future effectiveness by taking this little book seriously.

CHAPTER 1 — DISCUSSION QUESTIONS

1. What is the main reason this book encourages the reader to consider becoming a mental health professional?

2. What is the focus of clinical supervision?

3. What would you say is the most important thing a guide might do for you in your training process?

CHAPTER 2

WHAT IS CLINICAL SUPERVISION AND WHY IS IT IMPORTANT?

I F SUPERVISION IS AS IMPORTANT to your success as it sounds in Chapter One, then you should begin to understand it as soon as possible. That awareness prepares you to navigate the unfamiliar terrain of the world of mental health counseling and other forms of professional helping. An assertive and proactive student handles the normal stress of graduate training more effectively than a student who is passive and hesitant. This chapter discusses the importance of supervision and some of the major elements present in a complete definition of supervision. It will illustrate how the process works by sharing two brief accounts of beginning students and their supervisors.

SUPERVISION IS THE *SINE QUA NON* OF THE TRAINING PROCESS

You may not have expected to be learning Latin in this book, but the words *sine qua non* accent an important point. The phrase sine qua non literally means "that without which." Supervision is "that without which" not much happens in a clinical training program. In other words, a training program without clinical supervision would fall very short in its ability to prepare helping professionals for real-world careers. Why? Supervision provides an interface between more experience and less experience. It takes place at all the times and places where an experienced mental health professional (supervisor) meets the altruism, the curiosity, the compassion, and the professional ambition of a novice mental health professional.

Conveying practical knowledge is absolutely essential in any apprenticeship model that calls for a more experienced person to pass along valuable information to a less experienced person. There are many kinds of knowledge. In a clinical training program, knowing *how* to do something is as important as knowing *about* something. Every conversation you have with anybody related to the training program amounts to creating and sharing knowledge together. Very little is wasted in a good training program where everyone wants to support and to learn from everybody else. The best counselors and psychotherapists never stop learning.

IT'S NORMAL TO FEEL OVERWHELMED IN THIS KIND OF TRAINING PROGRAM

You may already sense that learning to master all the things that make for clinical competence can make you a little nervous sometimes. Okay, the truth is it can make you *a lot* nervous sometimes. Remember: You are not alone. Supervision matters to most beginning students who feel overwhelmed by the prospect of learning how to practice psychotherapy. In other words, feeling overwhelmed is normal at certain points in the training process. A supervisor's job is to help you manage this anxiety so that it energizes and motivates you to keep going until you feel more confident.

A central perspective in this book, and one that will seem a little radical to some, encourages a new role for the beginning student in a clinical training program. That new role helps the student cope with the anxiety normal for graduate-level clinical training. If we are always learning from each other, there is little room for the "blank slate" kind of student who expects to be hand-fed like a captive animal in a zoo. Think about what your reaction might be to the following questions: What difference would it make if students were encouraged from the beginning to be proactively engaged in the process of supervision? What if students could feel empowered and assertive in their roles as learners? What if this attitude helped you to more confidently integrate all the things that make for clinical competence?

Now what happened to the feeling of anxiety we were talking about just a minute ago? If you detect a slight lessening of what seemed overwhelming, you understand one of the main points I want to make in this little book. You are a worthy participant in this new endeavor. You will be a welcomed new member in the family of mental health professionals. You are not alone. In short, you get to relax and count on the fact that if you engage the learning process with as much energy as you can muster, you not only will succeed, you will be helping others succeed as well—including the supervisors. It doesn't get any better than that.

WHAT IS SUPERVISION ANYWAY?

The role of supervision and of the supervisor comes into sharper focus when seen as part of the whole transformative learning process. Supervision usually takes the shape of a dialogue with an experienced therapist to whom a student therapist endeavors to bring together all that she/he has learned and has become as a result of the professional socialization process. Everything is part of that socialization process that transforms the curious student therapist into a confident, competent professional. Everything encourages integration of everything else. The process of integration energizes the student's ability to imagine herself or himself as a developing competent professional. The student's inner voice begins to say more and more confidently, "I can do this. I want to do this well." That attitude of determined confidence makes for an effective helping professional.

A complete definition of supervision will include references to: a context, a relationship, a conversation, a process, a set of goals, and a set of standards for competence. There are other possible elements of a definition, but these allow for a fairly comprehensive description of a complex process of socialization that begins with a student's first interest in becoming a mental health professional and, basically, never stops. Most students have not imagined the difficulty of a process that requires them to learn to synthesize academic instruction and clinical instruction into a workable whole.

A context. Supervision takes place in the context of a training regimen for future mental health professionals. Most students who plan to become licensed professionals are obliged to pursue a challenging structured course of study in an accredited training program before they can sit for a licensing exam. The fact that mental health professionals are licensed by the state implies a legal arrangement in which various professional associations promise to train future mental health professionals to meet the highest possible standards for competence. Those legal obligations quickly become ethical obligations for the professional associations and training programs responsible for ensuring that the professional socialization process takes place in a context of rigorous academic and clinical excellence.

A relationship. Supervision requires a relationship between a more experienced professional and a future, but less experienced, colleague. By relationship I mean that the two must relate to each other in some fashion to accomplish the requisite goals of supervision. This is a multi-tasking relationship, for sure. It is not always comfortable for either side. The supervisor not only conveys information, but also models how that information might influence a therapist's behavior or how it might influence the way a therapist thinks about the client. The supervisee-as-witness has no meaning apart from a relation to the supervisor-as-mentor.

The supervisee relates to the supervisor as an apprentice would relate to a master practitioner (except that few experienced therapists would describe themselves as masters).

A conversation. If supervision is a relationship, then it is also a conversation or a dialogue in which two or more people share the very human project of making sense of things. Just because one may know a little (or even a lot) more than the other does not mean only one person gets to talk. Human beings construct reality together in conversation. The Oxford scholar Rom Harre (1983) suggests that "the primary human reality is persons in conversation." In the give and take of that conversation, new horizons are defined and explored as both student and supervisor together make sense of the student's developing competence. Social constructionists believe that we co-create reality together more or less continually in conversation. We are constantly testing and deconstructing old meanings while at the same time creating new meanings that might work better.

A process. Supervision refers to a sequence of unique events that function as links in a chain, each one of which enhances and strengthens the one before and the one after. Supervision, therefore, also describes an ongoing process in which an initial experience takes on greater meaning in light of all subsequent experiences. Once a student learns how to do skill A, he or she is more open to recognizing the value and relevance of skill B, and so on. In other words, the supervision process becomes a transformative process similar to the ideal for the therapy process. This process consists of each and every learning moment that takes place at any point along the transformative continuum. It might involve a faculty member and it might not. A great deal of essential learning takes place in small groups and in private conversations without a faculty member present.

A set of goals. The students already realize that there is a point to all the academic material with which they are inundated during the early phases of training. The problem is that there are multiple ways to talk about this point. What is the goal of training? Is it the same as the goal of supervision? Do they coincide or overlap? How is one integrated into the other? Most of these questions amount to the student's unspoken questions: What is going to happen to me along the way? How will I be different as I approach the goal of the training process? Lerner (2008) suggests that the goal of supervision ought to be assisting students as they move toward a sense of professional identity. Who can argue with the suggestion that *self-supervision* is a good way to describe the universal goal of supervision? Others remind us that "a key goal of supervision is to ensure that clients receive competent, ethical services" (Herlihy, 2006, p. 18). Some believe that the main goal is to develop the ability to listen to oneself while listening to the other. Another program might frame the goal as a way-of-being in conversation or a way of managing a certain kind of conversation. You will learn aspects of all of these things.

A set of standards for competence. In recent years, the mental health profession has begun to experiment with a new way of thinking about how to measure success in the delivery of psychotherapeutic services involving the use of "core competencies."

This new way of thinking directly impacts the education of future therapists. Required for effective performance, a competency is a professional skill that can be measured and verified. To take just one example, in 2002 several outstanding academics and practitioners connected to the American Association for Marriage and Family Therapy (AAMFT) formed a task force to discuss the pros and cons of identifying core competencies for the profession. The Core Competencies can be found on the AAMFT website.

In the end, the task force identified 128 core competencies (the first draft contained 270!) organized under the following six domains and five subdomains:

Domains	Subdomains
Admission to treatment	Conceptual skills
Clinical assessment and diagnosis	Perceptual skills
Treatment planning and case management	Executive skills
Therapeutic interventions	Evaluative skills
Legal issues, ethics, and standards	Professional skills
Research and program evaluation	

AAMFT is not the only organization taking the idea of core competencies seriously.

SANDY AND THE RECOVERING ALCOHOLIC

Sandy is a thirty-two year old educator who has seen enough of what students bring to the classroom to know that she wants to be able to work with the families who send those children to school. She is in a second-year practicum with five other students in her training program. She has been able to work with Emilio, a twenty-eight year old mechanic, who has been court-ordered to get counseling for the chronic drinking problem that figures into his third DUI (driving under the influence). While Emilio is embarrassed and angry about having to get counseling, he is also aware that his behavior threatens to undermine everything he has worked for in his life. He has grown a small mechanic shop into a successful operation with four other employees. Why work that hard, he thinks to himself, and then throw it all away because of alcohol?

Sandy, on the other hand, has strong feelings about alcoholism, because it figured in the early death of her grandfather who died of liver disease related to heavy drinking. Her supervisor reminds her before the second session with Emilio that it is okay for her to have mixed feelings about working with an alcoholic. Her experience might also motivate her to help Emilio. The supervisor also asks Sandy what skill she thinks will be most important in helping Emilio. She answers that besides careful listening, she must help him discover how his life might be different if it was not dominated by the effects of drinking alcohol. The supervisor smiles knowing that Sandy has been putting in some extra time reading about Narrative Therapy, in which the therapist externalizes the problem while helping the client write a new life story.

GREG'S STRUGGLE WITH A TROUBLED TEENAGER

Greg is a forty-two year old military veteran who is completing his internship year at a local psychiatric hospital where he is supervised by an experienced social worker known for her insights into how young mental health professionals learn. Greg has been working with Keisha, a fifteen year old who has a history of uncontrollable frustration and anger with her family members and at school. Keisha was arrested at school for hitting another student hard enough to send her to the hospital. The prosecutor in the case offered Keisha the opportunity to go to a facility where she could learn to manage her behavior. So far, she has alienated just about everybody in charge of her care. Except Greg. For some reason Keisha trusts Greg because he is not afraid of her. She asked him once, "Why aren't you afraid of me? Everybody else is." Greg answered, "How does it help when people are afraid of you?" Tears came to Keisha's eyes as she confessed that she feels so lonely she wants to die. She doesn't really know why God made her so mean.

Greg reports to his supervisor that Keisha seems to want to give him a chance, but he doesn't understand why Keisha trusts him. "Why do you think she wants to trust you, Greg?" his supervisor asks. Greg thinks for a minute and replies, "There must be some small part of her that is still healthy, that wants to be different." He and his supervisor talk about how compounding family traumas can shape a child's identity when that role only separates them from the love and security needed for healthy development. They discuss the fact that Keisha is taking some powerful medications that may also be affecting her behavior. Together they make adjustments to Keisha's treatment plan to give Greg more time with her for individual psychotherapy.

CONCLUSION

The main point of this book is that, like Sandy and Greg, you will not be alone if you decide to take on the difficult challenge of becoming a competent mental health professional. A lot of future clients unknown to you at this point are counting on the fact that you will take your training commitment seriously. "All excellent things are as difficult as they are rare." By accepting the challenge, you will join a host of other people whose journeys will enhance and enrich your own, even as you do the same for them.

If there is one thing on which all the books about supervision agree, it is that clinical supervision is important. Since the days of Freud, who believed that supervision must be as personal as possible, supervision has continued to be the primary method of training mental health professionals. There are myriad ways to conduct that task, but there seems no way around the need for some sort of master-apprentice relationship, no matter how uncomfortable it sometimes can be for both master and apprentice. Some discomfort is normal and can motivate you to keep moving toward the goal of feeling more confident in your new role as a future professional helping person. Refuse to be discouraged. Work through the anxiety and confusion.

In the short chapters ahead I will discuss the roles of the student, the supervisor, the collaborative learning community, and the client in successful supervision. In addition, I will place emphasis on the concept of competence, which has become so vital to the effective teaching and learning process. The next chapter is all about you and what you bring to supervision.

CHAPTER 2 — DISCUSSION QUESTIONS

1. What role might the student play in maximizing learning while minimizing the normal anxiety of the training process?

2. What are the elements of a definition of supervision, and which one might be most challenging for you?

3. Which one of the clinical stories about Greg and Sandy touches you more and why?

CHAPTER 3

THE ROLE OF THE STUDENT IN SUCCESSFUL SUPERVISION

THE TWO DISTINCTIVE SUGGESTIONS I make in this book connect two goals you can begin working toward right now. The first is the advantage of learning about the importance of clinical supervision from the earliest possible moment. The second distinctive suggestion is the encouragement to engage the process of supervision *proactively and assertively*, without apology and without fear. A good supervisor functions as a reassuring guide for beginning students who quite naturally feel overwhelmed by the prospect of learning how to practice psychotherapy. Let me say again that feeling overwhelmed may be normal at certain points in the training process. A supervisor's job is to help you manage the anxiety so that it energizes and motivates you to keep going until you feel more confident.

But please do not wait for the supervisor to pour counseling wisdom in your ear. You must learn to take maximum responsibility for your own learning. You will get more out of supervision if you give yourself permission to be assertive and engaged in the process. Several questions encourage me to encourage you to take this approach. Take a second and recall your answers to these questions from the last chapter: What if you proactively engaged the process of supervision from the first possible moment? What difference would it make if you could feel empowered and assertive in your role as learner? How might this attitude help you more confidently integrate all the things that make for clinical competence? In truth, you may answer that you do not yet know what difference your attitude might make in your training. I remain convinced that the answers to each of those questions support my two distinctive points.

In this chapter I will encourage you *to take ownership of your training*. I will introduce you to a developmental approach to supervision that discusses the process in terms of various stages through which you will go as you learn to integrate everything into a workable synthesis. You will be a work-in-progress for quite some time. Be patient with yourself. I will discuss the importance of focusing your passion for learning to make the most of the collaborative learning process before distinguishing between personal learning attitudes and shared learning attitudes.

THE MAGIC OF TAKING RESPONSIBILITY FOR YOUR POTENTIAL

To consider the role of the student in successful supervision assumes the student has a role in his or her own success. Who is responsible for developing your potential? Look no further than the closest mirror for the answer. A Houston business owner nicknamed "Mattress Mack" has a speech he often delivers called, "If It Is to Be, It's Up to Me." I can think of other clichés like that. "If That's True, It's Up to You!" We could go on forever, right? Actually, this is quite serious. You would not have read this far unless you were the kind of person who takes personal responsibility for what you want to do with your life. How much potential do you think you have?

One thing I know with confidence at my age is that most young people have more potential than they can yet imagine. The same is true for more mature folks as well. That's both cruel and exciting, because people waste their potential all the time. Why? Because they never knew they had any potential to develop. It's also exciting when one realizes the truth of that important proposition. You have more potential than you know. But you will need to patiently and resiliently develop it in order to see it for yourself. Mark it down, please: *The way you engage the training process is the way you will engage clients later.* First you learn to develop your own potential. Then you learn to help others develop theirs.

THE JOURNEY WILL TAKE YOU THROUGH SEVERAL DEVELOPMENTAL STAGES

Where do we begin? We should probably begin with the end in mind, as Stephen Covey (1989) says in his classic book, *The Seven Habits of Highly Effective People.* Habit Two in Covey's schema encourages the reader interested in developing potential to begin with a long-range goal or vision of the future. Think about it for a minute. What do you find compelling about your dreams of being a highly effective counselor or psychotherapist? There is something about that kind of gratification that seems to make one's work meaningful and rewarding. What makes you think the trip will be worth the trouble? This journey will not be easy. I promise you. What could possibly motivate you to tolerate all the sacrifices required to succeed both academically and clinically to graduate from a training program? There must be a clear destination to make the journey bearable. There ought to be observable markers that guide you along the way to your ultimate goal.

That's pretty easy in terms of supervision for the beginning mental health professional as she winds her way through various developmental stages toward a state of readiness to begin working with clients. Supervisors tend to think in terms of developmental theory about how things progress in a clinical training program because it provides a map for getting to the destination. Students tend to evolve through fairly predictable stages from the fired-up beginner to the nervous, but still striving student in stage two to the more relaxed and more confident student in stage three. In other words, if you begin at Level 1 (Stoltenberg & Delworth, 1987) in the training process, what will you be like at Level 3? As you might suspect, one is less anxious, more collaborative with clients, more relaxed and more creative in the effective use of oneself as an agent of change for the client. I still get a kick out of watching students evolve.

A student at Level 3 works with the client's emotional impact on the therapist, but also understands how the client's thoughts and feelings impact the client's life. The work begins to look like real therapy. The Level 3 student who survived the storms of levels 1 and 2 is recovering something of her early motivation, but with a hard-earned wisdom that comes from integrating various experiences into an evolving personal therapeutic style. The Level 3 student has learned enough self-confidence to work more or less independently from the supervisor. He or she also knows what to do in the event of feeling stuck or confused about what to do next. These are early glimpses of a vital lifelong openness to consultation with colleagues and other professionals.

The problem with talking this way about what kind of student you will be at Level 3 is that you obviously have to go through Levels 1 and 2 to get there. The stages are not nearly as neat and clean as I make them sound. However, everything between the first stages of training and the closing stages of training fit together in an overall plan designed to help you make sense of things as you go along. Your relationship with your supervisor will often reflect the intricacies as well as the tensions of the various movements. You will find yourself integrating things into a unified skill set that will allow you to function smoothly and effectively without having to think about everything you're doing. If there is a method to the madness, then what attitudes will give you the best chance for success?

WHAT ATTITUDES ARE IMPORTANT FOR MAXIMIZING YOUR POTENTIAL?

The father-daughter team Allen and Tanya Hess (2008) place at the top of their advice to beginning supervisees: *Take an active role.* On one hand, I must encourage you to take responsibility for your own learning. On the other hand, I want to reassure you that you are not alone in the training process. You will work not only with various instructors and supervisors, but also with other students who will share the journey with you. The proactive attitude fits with the best of collaborative learning approaches that focus on the shared responsibility of all learners, including faculty members. By the way, the attitude of collaborative learning is what makes for successful therapy. For now at least, focus on yourself and your own growth.

Collaborative learning is sometimes called Type Three Learning (Peters & Armstrong, 1998). It is a new model for maximizing one's potential by maximizing group learning.

Peters and Armstrong (1998) point out that Type Three learning can be frustrating to students who find themselves in a situation where they are expected to take maximum responsibility for their own learning as well as their contributions to the learning of others in the group. Students often feel like the teacher is suddenly changing the rules of the game. I predict you will rapidly learn to value collaborative learning.

What attitudes crucial to your success are implied in the multiple roles you will play in a collaborative learning environment? There are both *personal learning attitudes and shared learning attitudes* that combine to ensure the success of supervision and your success as a mental health professional. Those two kinds of attitude overlap quite often, creating a kind of synergy that seems to accelerate both personal learning and group learning. As the individual learns to share his learning, the group learns from him. As the group learns from him, he learns from the group.

PERSONAL LEARNING ATTITUDES

1. Openness to learning

Earlier in this book, I mentioned the saying, "When a student is ready to learn, a teacher will appear." Everything depends on one's openness to being confronted and impacted by new information. I often compare it to what military people go through in basic training. They don't want to do it, but they know they must in order to survive the worst situations. Allowing yourself to grapple with ideas that don't immediately make sense can test your nerves. On the other hand, if you begin with humility and appreciation for the hard-earned wisdom of more experienced colleagues, you will be on the lookout for anything and everything you can gather that might help you learn and integrate it all into a workable synthesis called clinical competence.

2. Passionate curiosity about everything related to helping people

Learning how to help people professionally requires a serious commitment to an almost overwhelming responsibility. Clients give mental health professionals a great deal of power to influence them at vulnerable moments in their lives. Like it or not, the client wants to trust you. A calloused or know-it-all counselor can harm the client at exactly the moment when the client most desperately needs help. Remember the Hippocratic Oath? The most well-known part says, "At least do no harm." That's why it is vital for an aspiring mental health professional to commit to a passionate curiosity about whatever it takes to manage that overwhelming responsibility with the greatest amount of care and skill. What makes people tick? How have other counselors and psychotherapists learned to help people? What new insights seem to be emerging from current research? Make sure you find ways to feed your eagerness to know as much as you can about all of it.

3. A philosophical attitude toward uncertainty and ambiguity

Working with people is not like working a math problem. Life contains confusing and tragic elements that leave the most philosophical of us scratching our heads. When a mental health professional finds a way to be helpful to a couple with a painfully entangled mess of a relationship, life will usually continue to be a painfully entangled mess for them on occasion. We do what we can to help people when they are stuck, but we do not hope to be able to play God and fix things forever. A mature mental health professional accepts that working with other human beings takes place against a backdrop of uncertainty and ambiguity. From one session to the next we can never be sure what might happen by the time we see the client. When human beings attempt to solve problems through language, the job is never finished. We are always "works in progress." Learn to be okay with things feeling messy and incomplete.

4. Patience with oneself in the developmental process

In my teaching, I have often come close to getting on my knees and begging beginning students to be patient with themselves. It probably wouldn't work, but I really wish it did. Remember that these kinds of skills require a lot of time and experience to master, if anyone ever masters them. Competence in psychotherapy demands a level of integration unlike almost every other profession. While a beginning student displays ideal characteristics of high motivation, that student might also experience a great deal of anxiety about what they do not yet know. Most training programs place a premium on being able to make effective use of feedback from supervisors and even other students. Be radically open to coaching and any kind of feedback you can get your hands on. But also remember to be patient with yourself in the process. You will get there. Give it time.

5. Perseverance to keep up with all the reading involved

I warned you before, and I will warn you again: Becoming a skilled practitioner who finds creative ways to be helpful to clients will not be easy. Diamonds take time. Let me come at it this way: What is your goal? Are you willing to do what it takes to get there? Graduate-level training to become a mental health professional requires graduate-level reading. You will spend a lot of time reading books and articles, not to mention reading and re-reading the papers you will be writing as you crystallize your thoughts. You will learn how to manage it, mainly because you have to learn how to manage it to avoid feeling overwhelmed. Otherwise you might never have time to sleep or do much of anything else. Every page you read is like the brush stoke of a master painter who works to capture your portrait as a mental health professional.

6. A positive attitude toward the unknown

Believe it or not, an experienced therapist requires the unknown to be successful. This may sound strange since we often talk about the fear of the unknown. The future remains radically open, full of promise and possibility. It is the realm of the "not-yet-said," as hermeneutic philosophers call it. Without the unknown there is no room for clients to experiment with new behaviors. Without the unknown, clients who already believe there is no hope would be right to give up on life. But because human beings are always in the process of co-creating and co-constructing the future together, there will always be room to do it another way. When you engage supervision with passionate eagerness to succeed, you participate in the creation of your therapist self as someone who will know how to use the unknown to help people.

7. A spiritual groundedness that helps you recover from anxiety and disappointment

"Spiritual" in this sense does not mean religious. It means a student's ability to develop oneself on deep levels that grow and mature while the student evolves and develops on other levels more closely related to behavioral and cognitive skills. One must learn to take care of oneself on this deep level to be able to tolerate the nervousness and discouragement that inevitably come. These emotions do not indicate a problem. On the contrary, they indicate that someone wishes she or he was further along in the normal developmental process of becoming a mental health professional. Find ways to nurture yourself like exercise or meditation. Many students pray or have an active role in a church, synagogue, or mosque. Humanist students find inspiration in art or nature. I always encourage beginning students to get into therapy for themselves somewhere along the way, even if for just a few sessions. It gives you a sense of what it might be like for those you hope to help someday. Learn to love and accept yourself just the way you are!

SHARED LEARNING ATTITUDES

1. Openness to learning from, with, and for others

It's one thing to say, "When a student is ready to learn, a teacher will appear." But what if that teacher is another student? Or what if that teacher is a client or client family? Readiness to learn requires a radical openness to the whole learning environment. As I will discuss later, in one sense supervision is going on all the time—if you are open to believing it. You will be learning not only *from* others, but also *with* others. Groups learn just like individuals learn, but groups learn only if the group members participate fully in the learning process. Remember that you are learning for all the people you will one day be able to help professionally. It all begins here and now.

2. Passionate curiosity about knowledge generated in dialogue with others

Knowledge is a social construction. We generate knowledge in the back and forth of conversation. The passionate, motivated graduate student will make sure to be involved in lots and lots of conversation while in the training process. Talk to everybody and anybody. More than discovering or being told what to believe, students create the knowledge they need to move from one developmental stage to the next. That commitment to meaningful dialogue prepares you to be able to do the same thing with clients.

3. A philosophical attitude toward the imperfections of shared learning

Shared learning is not a perfect process, because imperfect human beings are involved. Learning to work with clients begins with learning to work with professors, supervisors, and other students. Nobody has any of this nailed down. Everybody comes to the training process with ample room for improvement. You will be disappointed along the way. Believe it. Your deficits become strengths only as you embrace the imperfections and deficits of those with whom you share the change process of a training program. Isn't that what will be required when you work with the other hurting human beings called clients? Remember that the word "philosophy" comes from two Greek words which mean "love of wisdom." A philosophical attitude requires that you choose to love the wisdom of maturity-as-personal-commitment.

4. Perseverance to stay engaged with academic content and the interpersonal aspects of shared learning

You may already be able to imagine that one of the key elements of success in a graduate training program is perseverance. To get to the goal, just keep going. Don't quit. Don't even consider quitting. Just because you feel discouraged does not mean you are doing anything wrong. It may mean you are doing exactly what must be done. There will be times when you will get sick of all the reading and thinking about counseling psychology. You may get sick of the people with whom you share the journey of academic and clinical training. Choose to stay engaged. That's right. Choose it. Determine it. Hunker down and dig in. Do not quit! There is a method to the madness, I promise. The only way to appreciate the wisdom of advanced clinical training is to get to the end of it as you begin the integration process in earnest.

5. A positive attitude toward the always emerging new knowledge in the creative process of shared learning

A radical openness to learning equals openness to the not-yet-said, the constantly emerging knowledge being generated in the dialogue of training. Having a positive attitude toward that kind of collaborative learning makes it easier to integrate what fits perfectly into the gaps of your own personal learning. Listen eagerly. Consider everything. Challenge your defensiveness. In short, do everything in your power to open yourself as deeply as possible to the knowledge in which you will be immersed. Remember that you are involved not only in your own learning, but also the process of group learning. Your attitude toward shared learning either adds to or takes away from the learning of the group. There is no middle or neutral position. In my view, participation in shared learning is one of the early ethical responsibilities of a future mental health professional to take responsibility for the profound ways in which we are constantly influencing and being influenced by each other.

6. A shared spiritual groundedness that nurtures one's commitment to the others in the transformation process of shared learning

Ditto everything that has been said so far about personal learning, but place it in the context of shared learning. The relational expertise required of counselors and therapists begins with the compassionate wisdom of commitment to the well-being of others with whom one shares the journey. Self-care and other-care are flip sides of the same coin. How do you justify your commitment to your own care without at the same time admitting the worthiness of others to the same thing? If I am deserving of receiving the gifts of shared learning, then so are every one of my colleagues and clients. If transformation is really possible, why would I want to keep it all to myself? The truth is that change cannot be contained when it is time for it to occur. Future mental health professionals begin the training process with a moral commitment to doing everything within their power to amplify the possibility of transformation in every context of life.

CONCLUSION: WHAT MAKES YOU THE IDEAL STUDENT TO SUPERVISE?

Clinical supervision takes place in the context of a rigorous, structured training process with a more experienced colleague who will help you work toward the goal of becoming a competent mental health professional. It is the ultimate two-way street. The supervisor can only be as helpful as you are willing to be helped. He or she can only help you grow as much as you are open to personal and professional growth. So what makes for the ideal supervisee? What kinds of students make it fun and rewarding for the supervisor as well? I have discussed many of the characteristics of supervisees that supervisors rate as effective or desirable in their ability to contribute to successful supervision.

You will detect two recurring emphases in this book. The first encourages learning about the importance of supervision at the very beginning of training. The second emphasis grows out of a heartfelt encouragement that you *proactively* and *assertively* engage the process of supervision without apology and without fear. You are not alone. A good supervisor will help you navigate the often overwhelming prospect of learning how to do psychotherapy. Take responsibility for your own learning and for your role in the learning of the others with whom you share the training process. By doing so you will be preparing yourself to help future clients who will come to you desperately needing the kinds of skills you have already begun to develop.

CHAPTER 3 — DISCUSSION QUESTIONS

1. What is the main encouragement in this chapter?

2. Assuming each and every one of us has room to grow in the area of taking ownership of one's own learning, what will be different as you learn to do that?

3. Which attitudes for maximizing potential discussed in this chapter make most sense to you?

4. What will be most challenging for you in developing the shared-learning attitudes?

CHAPTER 4

THE ROLE OF THE SUPERVISOR IN SUCCESSFUL SUPERVISION

THE OTHER HALF OF THE supervisory relationship is the supervisor. We have talked about the role of the student in successful supervision in hopes of encouraging you to acquaint yourself with supervision from the beginning of your training and to engage the supervisory process with gusto and without fear or apology. In this chapter I will discuss with as much transparency as possible the role of the supervisor whose ideal role includes welcoming you into the profession as a future colleague while doing everything possible to acquaint you with the wide range of skills and responsibilities required of a mental health professional. The socialization process that transforms you into a professional helper will include everything else and everybody else involved in the process, but you will likely experience it first in the form of an instructor or supervisor.

Since nothing is to be gained by concealing the supervisor's goals and motives, it will help you understand the whole training process better if you understand the ideal role of the supervisor. Most instructors and supervisors will agree with the vision presented here. First, the supervisor's top priority is you and your success in the program. Supervision is a complex dialogical relationship. Start by assuming that your supervisor will like you and give you as much feedback as you can handle. Start by determining to embrace your supervisor's intention to mold you into a fully functioning mental health professional. Remember that your openness to learning determines how much of the supervisor's influence rubs off on you. Make a conscious choice to take complete responsibility for your contribution to that collaboration.

Second, supervisors wear many hats in their relationship with you. The ideal supervisor can make a chameleon blush in a competition for who can change colors faster. You will learn about some of those hats, including the ones you will learn to wear, as you progress in your training. And third, supervision as an ethical responsibility of the whole family of mental health practitioners is always on the supervisor's mind. Before we can stamp the good seal of approval on your forehead, we have to make sure we have done everything we can to prepare you for the tasks ahead. The roles of evaluator and gatekeeper add a level of difficulty hard to imagine for a beginning student. Not everyone is suited to become a mental health professional. Sometimes supervisors have to help students face the fact that they may do better in another field.

Your supervisor is The One Who Is Responsible. In other words, the responsibility for oversight of the transformative learning experience that takes place in a training program may be shared by all participants to some extent, but the supervisor plays an important leadership role by articulating the vision, the goals, and the parameters of the program. It is not an easy job. Instructors and supervisors not only function as living examples of the goals and values of the training program, but they also embody a performance of some of the key values and skills for students' consideration. There are more of these than you might think. Discussing supervisor competencies, Jane Campbell (2006) lists fourteen supervision skills essential to successful supervision, including knowledge of basic functions to knowledge of models, methods, and techniques, to awareness of requirements and procedures for obtaining a professional license.

THE ROLE OF THE SUPERVISOR IN THE SUPERVISORY RELATIONSHIP

The kind of relationship you have with your supervisor can color everything that happens during your time with that supervisor. The moral of that story may be to make sure you have more than one supervisor. But for sure the main thing to remember is to take responsibility for making the relationship as healthy and productive as possible. If it is true that supervision is "the major means of transmission of the foundations of the psychology profession to students, trainees, and supervisees" (Falender & Shafranske, 2012, p. vii), then your relationship with the person who transmits all that wisdom matters. Do your part to make your experience what you need for it to be. Chances are the supervisor already wants as much or more for you than you can imagine, even if he or she seems distracted by many other things. So be a good listener from your earliest contact with instructors and supervisors. You may be wondering about who is responsible for what.

Experts tend to agree with the premise that successful supervision must be relational and dialogical. In his concluding thoughts at the end of his handbook, Watkins (1997) reported that he had become, as a result of editing the handbook on supervision, even more convinced of the importance of a *relational training process* during which students learn about basic skills and quality service. Clinical supervision, says Watkins (1997, p. 603), "transmits, protects, and enhances a valuable culture, the culture of psychotherapy." It is the whole profession whose self-monitoring requires a close, personal, ongoing dialogue with each and every student in the program, each one of whom is a potential candidate for membership in the professional family.

That vital dialogue invites the less experienced future colleague (student) into a relationship with a more experienced colleague (supervisor). Note that from the beginning you will be a *colleague* of instructors and supervisors. Act like one! But understand that this more experienced colleague is there to provide guidance to help you become the best helping professional that you can be.

There has been a great deal of research and reflection on the supervisory relationship. One definition of supervision (Bernard and Goodyear, 1992) focuses on the relationship angle, calling it "an intervention" (p. 4), an action or behavior designed to influence someone.

Supervision is an intervention that is provided by a senior member of a profession to a junior member or members of that same profession. This relationship is evaluative, extends over time, and has the simultaneous purposes of enhancing the professional functioning of the junior member(s), monitoring the quality of professional services offered to the clients she, he, or they see(s), and serving as a gatekeeper for those who are to enter the particular profession. (Ibid.)

SUPERVISORS WEAR MANY HATS—CAN YOU?

The literature about the various roles played by supervisors almost always concludes by observing that supervisors wear a lot of hats in a training program. Take a minute to think about how many different kinds of things a supervisor might do. I have listed the following without much effort:

- Guide
- Educator
- Role model
- Conversation partner
- Encourager
- Coach
- Drill instructor (I didn't say it was all fun)
- Mentor
- Ethical conscience
- Co-learner

- Advisor
- Consultant

It might be fun to think of how many hats the student may be wearing in response to an evolving relationship with a supervisor with such an extensive wardrobe.

In his handbook, Hess (2008) delineates eight general roles played by supervisors. They include: lecturer, teacher, case reviewer, collegial peer, monitor, psychotherapist, coach, and educator. Each one has implications for the student's relationship with the supervisor. In one's relationship with the *lecturer* who introduces more global themes, one may choose to engage actively to learn as much as possible, but one may also be tempted to tune out and minimize the lecturer's input. In most of the roles, the student must adjust to being in a subordinate role requiring maximum openness and respect with maximum confidence and self-assertion. The role of the *collegial peer,* however, encourages a more relaxed positioning of oneself in the relationship with the supervisor to include shared closeness and trust. In direct contrast with the collegial peer, the *monitor* must function as one who can censure and correct the student who will, naturally, make mistakes along the way. Remember, you do not have to already know this stuff. How can you? Be patient with yourself and allow the process to work its magic. You will not regret it.

Roles require skills. Campbell (2006, p. 9) recommends the following skills for supervisors who dare to embrace the various roles of supervisor. See if you think these skills make sense for one who intends to play all the roles outlined above:

- *Knowledge in the areas of practice—group, individual, family, couple, child and adolescence*

- *Relationship skills—ability to build rapport and trust*

- *Ethical judgment and decision-making*

- *Knowledge and application of ethical guidelines and standards to specific cases and situations, particularly in crisis*

- *Crisis management skills*

- *Assessment and diagnostic skills*

- *Conceptualization skills*

- *Problem-solving and goal-setting skills*

- *Knowledge and experience in the use of the methods and techniques of counseling and psychotherapy*

- *Intervention strategies*—knowledge and application of a variety of intervention techniques for change

- *Written skills*—documentation and record-keeping

- *Knowledge of and ability to understand systems and the interaction between individuals, setting, environmental factors, and presenting problems*

- *Knowledge of multicultural issues and ability to respond to those issues*

- *Understanding of the role of developmental factors in client problems*

See what I mean? Who would want a job with so many different expectations? Answer: the person who will be your supervisor. Try to appreciate the complexity of his or her responsibility.

If roles require skills, then skills require behavioral embodiment. Effective supervisors endeavor to consistently model certain behaviors in their relationships with students. This is the part where a supervisor attempts to embody a performance of key values and skills for students' consideration. A lot of this kind of learning is indirect and experiential as one's relationship with the supervisor evolves.

Campbell (2006, p. 11-12) again provides a concise summary of effective supervisory behaviors:

- *Clarifies expectations and roles*
- *Is accessible and available*
- *Is able to create a safe learning environment*
- *Has the ability to communicate effectively*
- *Models appropriate ethical behavior*
- *Is personally and professionally mature*
- *Has an awareness of personal power*
- *Has a sense of humor and does not take himself or herself too seriously*

Now that you know some of what supervisors intend to model for you, see if you can catch them in the act of showing you how a mental health professional behaves.

As you imagine the kind of supervisor you would like to have, take care to avoid imagining your nightmare version of the supervisor that you would hate to have. Self-fulfilling prophecies are the worst kind of self-sabotage. Inform your positive expectations and be prepared to work with that kind of supervisor. She or he is only human. If you consciously or unconsciously prepare yourself for a negative experience, you will find yourself having to play catch-up in the most important area of your training. Often a positive relationship with one's supervisor can have a deep therapeutic effect on a student, even though one is not in therapy with the supervisor. Grab all the healing and transformation you can get your hands on. It will help you understand a client's craving for the same experience.

BEAR AND SHARE: AN ETHICAL RESPONSIBILITY OF THE WHOLE FAMILY OF MENTAL HEALTH PROFESSIONALS

I have been struck by the extent to which supervision is an ethical responsibility of the whole family of mental health professionals. Remember: you are not alone. Sperry (2007) points out in his book on ethics, "For most counselors and therapists the process of becoming competent to engage in professional practice begins with graduate training" (153). Therefore, Sperry continues, "graduate faculty and supervisors bear the initial responsibility for producing competent professionals." Are you prepared to participate in that responsibility? This is a bear and share kind of relationship. Everyone bears part of the load, and everyone shares the burden of that bearing.

Any of the websites dedicated to professional associations such as the American Association for Marriage and Family Therapy, the American Psychological Association, etc. will detail the importance of training and supervision. These statements indicate the importance experienced professionals attach to the socialization of younger or less experienced colleagues into the field. State laws and codes of ethics amount to promises made to the public that licensed professionals will accept, train, evaluate, weed out, and supervise future professionals toward the goal of protecting future clients and patients from possible harm. Are you beginning to see how much responsibility the supervisor has to manage?

If the whole community of mental health professionals bears responsibility for the socialization of future mental health professionals, then there must be important ethical reasons for taking that responsibility as seriously as possible. This responsibility grows out of a *commitment to self-monitoring* reflected in the various state licensing acts and the codes of ethics of various professional associations. The public hears this commitment as a promise to provide services aimed at "helping without hurting" (Pope and Vasquez, 2007), including guarantees that candidates for licensure have participated in a rigorous training experience designed to equip them for maximizing help while minimizing harm.

To some degree, licensing acts and codes of ethics give us ways of talking about the goals of our training programs, but those documents often couch the therapist's responsibilities in negative language or in minimalist terms. However, as discussed in Chapter 2, the American Association of Marriage and Family Therapy has suggested the use of Core Competencies for training and evaluation purposes. Falender and Shafranske (2004) introduced what they call "a competency-based approach" to supervision.

They (Falender & Shafranske, 2012) invented a Competency Cube to enhance the learning of essential knowledge, skills, and attitudes. In addition, common factors research (Duncan, Miller & Sparks, 2004) allows clinicians an increasingly interesting glimpse into the client's expectations with clear implications not only for effective therapy, but also for effective supervision.

At some point the student must embrace that same commitment to integrated trustworthiness promised to the public by the whole community of professional helpers. One's relationship with a supervisor is usually one's first point of contact with this vital aspect of becoming a mental health professional. Embracing the values of the profession as channeled through a supervisor may be the essential first step in the transformative journey from novice to competent clinician. You will learn that one must develop not only in a way that makes sense to oneself, but also in a way that makes sense to others. Those others will ultimately include the public, i.e. the clients and patients for whom one will provide responsible care.

CONCLUSION

One idea keeps coming to my mind as I introduce you to the multifaceted world of the supervisor: none of it means anything without you. That relationship must become a dialogical relationship to reach maximum effectiveness. The role of the supervisor in successful supervision is a meaningless abstraction without your engagement and participation in the supervisory relationship.

Your supervisor knows this. You will be welcomed, nurtured, and encouraged in the training process, even if you have a negative experience on occasion. You may not always be the center of attention, but you will be encouraged to succeed and nurtured in the process.

In this chapter I have tried to give you a glimpse into the supervisor's world. First and foremost, supervision is a relational experience. That relationship is actually your first relationship with clients in one sense, because the way you think about and interact in supervision says a lot about the kinds of relationships you will have with the clients who come to you for help. Second, I wanted you to begin to understand the dizzying array of hats supervisors must wear in order to contribute to your full socialization into the family of mental health professionals. If it sometimes feels like an impossible set of expectations, be patient with yourself as well as the process. It will make more and more sense as you integrate the influence of that relationship into your developing professional identity. Finally, I want you to see as much of the big picture as you can handle in terms of the ethical responsibility taken on by faculty and supervisors who willingly accept the often risky role of preparing you for presentation to the world as a trustworthy provider of competent care.

CHAPTER 4 — DISCUSSION QUESTIONS

1. What is unique about the kind of relationship this chapter encourages you to develop with your supervisor?

2. What impression do you have now of all the different things supervisors are expected to be able to do?

3. What are some of the implications of the section on how to manage the moral responsibility of training future mental health professionals?

CHAPTER 5

THE ROLE OF THE COLLABORATIVE LEARNING COMMUNITY IN SUCCESSFUL SUPERVISION

PERHAPS YOU CAN ALREADY SENSE that if you follow through on your dream of being a mental health professional, you will be involved in the lives and learning of a lot of other people, including instructors. In the introduction I pointed out that you will be joining a huge community of people from all walks of life who see the tremendous need for competent, highly skilled professional helpers in today's society. Any training program amounts to a sub-community within the larger one that will welcome you and also prepare you for membership in the larger family of mental health professionals. Supervisors and instructors represent that larger community as they attempt to interpret the novel elements of the training process to a beginning student. They are your first points of contact not only with the larger community but also with your own dreams of being able to help people professionally. They will also welcome you into the world of collaborative learning.

In this chapter I will introduce you to a new way of talking about the ideal training program. I promised that you would not be alone, and I intend to keep my promise (with your help, of course). Most programs include elements of a communal approach to the learning process even if they do not use the language of a collaborative learning community. In the same way that life itself is a radically relational experience, intensive clinical training can only be accomplished to the degree that it maximizes the contributions of everyone who participates in the process. Your commitment to your dream of being a helping professional now becomes a conscious and passionate commitment to the specific collaborative learning community that grants you admission into their training program. Give it your best.

A COLLABORATIVE LEARNING COMMUNITY?

My first exposure to this way of thinking was through the writing of my mentor and friend Dr. Harlene Anderson (1997, 1999, 2000, 2007), who has long been associated with the Houston Galveston Institute in Houston, Texas. Along with the late Harold Goolishian, Harlene has been an innovator in the field of psychotherapy in general and family therapy in particular. She writes about the profound implications of our radically social interrelatedness.

Anderson's compelling vision of a collaborative learning community emphasizes: (1) shared responsibility for learning, (2) dialogue as dynamic generative conversation in which there is room for all voices, and (3) transformation that occurs in and through dialogue. She likes to talk about the 3 Cs: Connect,

Collaborate, and Construct. If you will set your moral compass to automatically adjust to Connect, Collaborate, and Construct, you will succeed not only in reaching your personal goals, but also in helping others reach theirs. The values inherent in the vision of a collaborative learning community ought to inform any contemporary training program.

Anderson's work grows out of an innovation-inspiring interpretation of social constructionist assumptions. The tradition that winds its way back through Berger and Luckmann (1966) to George Herbert Mead (1934) and the influence of American pragmatism (Dewey, 1938; James, 1970; Menand, 1997, 2001), is most capably represented these days by Kenneth J. Gergen (1994, 1999, 2009), who has spent much of his career elucidating the various themes and vast implications of social constructionist ways of thinking.

In his more recent work Gergen (2009) builds on earlier assumptions, but continues to experiment with even more radical implications of what he calls relational being. "There is nothing that requires us to understand our world in terms of independent units; we are free to mint new and more promising understandings. As the conception of relational being is grasped, so are new forms of action invited, new forms of life made intelligible, and a more promising view of our global future made apparent" (Gergen, 2009, p. 5). One of those new forms of life would be experimenting with ways to maximize group learning. What might this imply for the role of the collaborative learning community in successful supervision?

DIFFERENT KINDS OF SUPERVISION WITHIN THE COLLABORATIVE LEARNING COMMUNITY

Faculty-directed supervision. One kind of supervision involves a faculty member and a student and sometimes more than one student. It is a narrower and more systematic approach to trainee socialization. This kind of supervision involves *direct faculty influence* as in the traditional case consultation format. In that format, the faculty member directs the conversational themes and more or less evaluates student progress by inviting the student to perform some newly acquired skill or integration of skills as a way of determining something about the student's developmental stage. This kind of supervision can be supportive and essential to the smooth integration of the million and one things students are supposed to integrate while in graduate school. Hopefully, the supervisor is wise enough to focus on what the student does well, allowing her or him to leave supervision feeling encouraged.

Faculty-directed supervision is the more traditional understanding of supervision and basically amounts to what is often called case consultation. In that kind of supervision, the student reviews a case with a supervisor who gives advice and makes suggestions about how to work more effectively with a particular client or family. That approach is also sometimes called "dead" supervision because of the absence of a client or clients. Live supervision, on the other hand, usually refers to supervision in which students and supervisor are in the presence of a client or clients.

Community-generated supervision. There is another kind of supervision that is much less directive, less conscious, and less specific, but has all the elements of competence-enhancing supervision. Community-generated supervision refers to all aspects of *indirect and informal faculty influence*. It takes place anytime, anywhere and involves just about anybody. It takes place in the informal conversations in the hallway between classes. It takes place in phone calls and in bars and in living rooms. This level of supervision amplifies the process of integration of faculty influence by means of conversations large and small about the meaning of that influence.

Community-generated supervision describes a broader and more systemic professional socialization process evolving in the midst of and as a result of the various "supervisory" aspects of all the program-inspired interactions between members of the collaborative learning community.

Social constructionist ways of thinking about how people create meaning together in the ongoing flow of interaction help us make the distinction between the two levels of supervision discussed above. Clearly, this distinction spreads accountability among all members of the learning community instead of assuming it rests completely with faculty and supervisors.

A LEARNING GROUP IN ACTION

Our friends Sandy and Greg belong to the same learning group in their training program. While their backgrounds could not be more different, they have learned to move past old prejudices and hesitations to participate in each other's professional (and even personal) development. On a particular night close to the holiday break, the group takes time to allow both Sandy and Greg to talk about the clients they are seeing in their internships. It does not seem to surprise anyone when Greg has tears in his eyes when he talks about one of his young clients at the hospital. While the others listen supportively, Greg manages to talk about how he must learn to handle the sadness of hearing client stories. Sandy almost declines to talk about her client because she is learning how to handle her disgust with the chronically irresponsible behavior of some of her alcohol and drug abuse clients. She is not sad; she is pissed off!

For the next two hours the team collaborates in the all-important process of sharing their experiences, thoughts, and feelings. All this is new to them, and they struggle to integrate it all into their developing sense of professional identity. The truth is that none of them really knows what to say to Greg or to Sandy, not only because they are all coping with the same issues, but also because they do not yet have enough experience to know what to expect. At this point, someone suggests, "Why don't we ask Dr. Smith to come talk to us about that?" At first they hesitate to agree, partly because they fear that Dr. Smith will judge them as incompetent therapists. "Dr. Smith warned us this would happen and told us to be patient with how troubling these experiences can be," Sandy exclaims, now with tears in her eyes as well. "Why does it have to be so damn hard?" Suddenly she starts laughing instead.

The others look at each other with concern. "I can hear him warning us that all excellent things are as difficult as they are rare." They all laugh, and for a moment the stress fades into the background.

MAY I INTRODUCE YOU TO SOME (ACADEMIC) PEOPLE?

John Dewey. What we now call collaborative learning has been around as long as human beings have lived in groups. It is nothing less than the key to survival. To live together requires group problem-solving and group solution-creation. In the twentieth century the American pragmatist philosopher and educator John Dewey began to challenge the authoritarian and often abusive approach to education popular in the nineteenth century. Dewey focused on the needs of the learner rather than the dissemination of taken-for-granted truths. He insisted that effective education must connect with the ordinary experience of the student. In Dewey's own words,

> It becomes the office of the educator to select those things within the range of existing experience that have the promise and potentiality of presenting new problems which by stimulating new ways of observation and judgment will expand the area of further experience (Dewey, 1938, p. 75).

Everything builds upon everything else.

Like many educators today, Dewey (1938) grieved the disillusionment with education that sent many bright minds fleeing from its lifeless clutches. "How many students," he asked (p. 26), "were rendered callous to ideas, and how many lost the impetus to learn because of the way in which learning was experienced by them?" In other words, how we learn and what we learn is inextricably connected. Dewey prophetically identifies the connection between relationships and a more democratic approach to education so important in later theory about collaborative learning. Education is basically a social process.

We can safely conclude from Dewey's extensive influence on American education that one's philosophy of education matters in terms of what it allows the student to create with other students, as well as the teacher, in a formal educational setting. In many ways, Dewey's vision has yet to be taken seriously in education generally. Such a commitment to democratic learning must incorporate a bold willingness to allow people to interact with each other and think out loud without fear of judgment or intimidation by some institutionally sanctioned expert (McNamee, 2007). The fact that there is more and more consensus about the effectiveness of collaborative learning is due in some measure to the work of several devoted educators who continue to herald the arrival of a practical and effective approach to learning in the spirit of John Dewey.

Kenneth Bruffee. In his work on collaborative learning, Bruffee (1999) begins with the assumption that "professors and students alike construct and maintain knowledge in continual conversation" (p. xi). One detects the influence of social constructionist assumptions in Bruffee's philosophy of education, which emphasizes the importance of what he calls "reacculturation," an encouragement to allow students to grow and transform as a result of the co-construction of knowledge in which they share. He also emphasizes the importance of the development of inter-dependence in the student. "With collaborative learning," Bruffee writes, "they learn to construct knowledge as it is constructed in the knowledge communities they hope to join after attending colleges and universities" (1999, p. xiii). Students learn to grow as they learn to think—together.

Bruffee (1999) draws a distinction between cooperative learning and collaborative learning, but notes that both share the idea that constructive conversation is an important part of the learning process:

> We claim that students learn by joining transition communities in which people construct knowledge as they talk together and reach consensus. What teachers do in both collaborative and cooperative learning is to set up conditions in which students can learn together. One of the most important ways teachers do that is by organizing students into transition communities for reacculturative conversation. (p. 84)

An educator's role, by this logic, is similar to that of a therapist: to help students learn to cope with the intellectual challenges faced by their experiences of confusion, ambiguity, and uncertainty.

In his chapter on education as conversation, Bruffee (1999) says that "education initiates us into conversation, and by virtue of that conversation initiates us into thought" (p. 133). In other words, the reason we can think at all is because we can talk to each other. Conversation transforms even the most individual tasks into collaborative ones. One of the most significant challenges facing college and university students is learning to speak in the new ways that accompany their field of interest. Specialized language challenges one to tolerate a good deal of stressful puzzling, both alone and with others who are also in the process of learning the language of a wider world or of a specialized discipline. Accompanying this learning of specialized languages and disciplines with one's peers also opens students up to challenges about their preconceptions and existing views of a particular subject. Bruffee (1999) writes:

> Most students didn't mind examining and demolishing other students' preconceptions. But few liked exposing their own preconceptions to examination and demolition by their peers. Finding exposure frustrating and painful, they tended—sometimes fiercely—to resist the changes that the process led to. At the same time, however, most students found that this mutually challenging conversation made revising their preconceptions almost inevitable. For most, it was relatively easy, when teachers had challenged their preconceptions, to shrug the challenge off, willfully misinterpret or defy it. When a peer challenged their preconceptions, the challenge tended to stick. (p. 145)

Transformative learning takes place in an environment in which uncontrolled, open dialogue is the norm.

John Peters and Joseph Armstrong. Peters and Armstrong (1998) identify a kind of collaborative learning in which "people labor together in order to construct something that did not exist before the collaboration, something that does not and cannot fully exist in the lives of individual collaborators" (p. 75). They talk about the synergy that occurs when people collaborate, contributing to the effort individually and jointly. Thus, individuals learn, but so does the group. The meanings attributed to all the various interactions depend a great deal on the kind of relationship the members have with one another because of the interactive nature of knowledge construction.

> In a group of collaborators, the group process moves from member to member, from member to group, and from group to member. Members don't just talk with one another. They also talk into the group and from the group. That is, as individuals talk to one another, they construct meaning from what is said and how it is said, and the result is meaning that the several people have constructed in the process of talking and interpreting, talking and interpreting, and so forth. What is jointly said and interpreted becomes the context for and the focus of further talk and interpretation. (p. 76)

This description brings to mind what happens in the dialogical relationships in a training program and the important role these relationships play in the construction of knowledge within the collaborative learning community.

One of the more interesting suggestions found in Peters and Armstrong (1998) is the delineation of three types of teaching and learning. Type One is the traditional student-as-passive-receptacle approach to education in which the expert instructor dispenses accurate knowledge to the blank-slate-minded student. In Type Two learning, teaching still takes place by transmission of knowledge, but it also includes learning in which students share the knowledge with each other and with the teacher. Type Three learning, on the other hand, is distinguished not only by a focus on joint construction of knowledge, but also by the designation of the teacher as a member of the group of learners and by the role of the group in the learning experience. The teacher is one of the participants in the collaborative learning experience. The teacher may and usually does have special knowledge of content, but his or her knowledge does not necessarily supersede that of the other learners in the group. (p. 79)

The instructor, in this way of thinking, must possess special skills as a facilitator of collaborative learning. Dialogue is the main way of sharing information in Type Three learning. Again, one hears language reminiscent of Anderson's (1999, 2000, 2007) description of a collaborative learning community.

Peters and Armstrong (1998) point out that Type Three teaching can be frustrating to students who find themselves in a situation where they are expected to take maximum responsibility for their own learning as well as their contributions to the learning of others in the group. Students often feel like the teacher is suddenly changing the rules of the game. The authors share the following ways in which they approach both undergraduate and graduate classes (pp. 82-83):

- We try to get students involved in an episode of collaborative learning as early in the course as possible.
- We take every opportunity to "point out" when we or others in the group are doing something to promote a collaborative learning experience.

- We try to show the utmost respect for everyone in the group and everything that is said by anyone in the group.

- We're not really sure whether trust follows respect or vice versa, but trust has to be in the mix along with respect.

- As facilitators, we have found that we need to know ever more content than we do as lecturers.

- As a course progresses, we try to facilitate what we call a "level-izing" process; that is, we want all of us to see ourselves learning, and to see ourselves seeing ourselves learning.

In general, Peters and Armstrong (1998) encourage educators and students to experiment with collaborative learning, but they also warn about the possibility of frustration because of the years of exposure to Type One and Type Two approaches to teaching.

CONCLUSION

If you succeed, and you will, it will not be alone. Does it help to know you are *immersed* in the training process? To be immersed in the systemic wisdom of a training community means that when you are radically open to anything and everything related to learning, you will inevitably absorb a lot of that systemic wisdom without even knowing it. You will responsibly and confidently engage faculty-directed supervision and you will profit from the more relaxed learning in community-generated supervision. When students participate fully in a collaborative learning community, they enhance the organic learning process for everyone. While you may want to write down "Connect, Collaborate, and

Construct" somewhere where you can see it often, remind the other members of your various learning groups to do the same. It might be a good time to review the discussion of personal learning attitudes and shared learning attitudes in Chapter 2. See if you can detect how they weave together into the tapestry of an evolving mental health professional.

CHAPTER 5 — DISCUSSION QUESTIONS

1. What is most unique about the notion of a collaborative learning community, in your opinion?

2. How might the distinction between faculty-directed supervision and community-generated supervision be useful to you?

3. What stands out as the most appealing aspect of collaborative learning for you?

CHAPTER 6

THE ROLE OF THE CLIENT IN SUCCESSFUL SUPERVISION

I T MAY SEEM OBVIOUS TO point out that "a key goal of supervision is to ensure that clients receive competent, ethical services" (Herlihy, 2006, p. 18). Why should we care about how supervision affects the client? The more intoxicating your graduate training becomes, the more important it is to recall the words of traditional clinical wisdom: Not much happens without the client! If I ask why you want to be a mental health professional, you would pretty quickly end up talking about the people you want to help. In other words, why you engage a challenging training process means "*for whom?*" The client is the "for whom" we are talking about. You are going to all this trouble to be helpful to other human beings who are often called "clients" in clinical practice. They might also be called consumers or patients, depending on the context.

The crucial question driving supervision is: How can I include the client in the therapy process in a way that is clearly beneficial to her or him? Ironically, until recently the person most likely to be missing in traditional literature about supervision was the client. Hard to believe, right? Recent outcome research makes clear that *as much as half* of what contributes to change comes from the client who is, after all, the one coming for help. Other factors include: relationship factors, model/technique factors, and placebo, hope, and expectancy. In other words, to say that not much happens without the client really means *nothing* happens without the client.

What attitude should you have toward the client? Does it really matter? What possible negative attitudes could you have toward a client? Is the client resistant? Lazy? Defiant? Out of control? Unworthy of your helping intentions? Unfortunately, students sometimes end up with the impression that the client is somehow "less than" the all-wise, all-knowing graduate student. Beware of that attitude. It is not only more likely to fail, but also more likely to be dangerous for the client. I often have the image of the graduate student as one who is dressed in camouflage, armed to the teeth with all the latest armor and weaponry, prepared to do battle with the darkest forces known to the human imagination. The client, meanwhile, sits in the waiting room shivering, starving, and half-naked. A worthy opponent indeed!

We cannot afford to lose sight of the client in the training process to become a mental health professional. You will eventually see the wisdom in the phrase "the client is the expert" (Anderson & Goolishian, 1992). The client plays the major role in successful supervision, even if the client is not present in the supervision conversation. The client is not the enemy, nor is the therapist a dragon-slayer. What is a better way of thinking about the person who is the client?

THE HEROIC CLIENT

One of the most important books for serious psychotherapists in recent years is *The Heroic Client: Doing Client-Directed Outcome-Informed Therapy* (Duncan & Miller, 2000), in which the authors introduce us to some of the implications of common factors research. That kind of research gives us insights into what actually makes counseling and psychotherapy effective across all models and approaches. First, the book debunks some of the time-honored myths about psychiatric diagnosis, pointing out that often: a) it lacks reliability, b) it lacks validity, c) it puts the blame on the client, and d) it is frequently influenced by self-interest, greed, and the winds of fashion.

The heart of the book focuses on how and why psychotherapy is more effective than drug treatment. The authors dig into what really makes change possible in any treatment situation. What contributes to change? If your goal is to help people by helping them change something they find problematic, would it not make sense to know in advance what variables are most highly correlated to change? Decades of outcome research have shown that there are four main factors of change:

1. Client factors: the strengths and resources clients bring to therapy (40% contribution to change)

2. Relationship factors: the quality of the therapeutic alliance between the therapist and the client (30% contribution to change)

3. Hope and expectancy: sometimes called the placebo effect, referring to the client's beliefs and hopes that therapy will help (15% contribution to change)

4. Model and technique: the use of a particular therapy approach to working with the client (15% contribution to change)

Note that the first two account for 70% of positive outcomes. What do these facts suggest?

The authors believe that "to end the medievalism that has both characterized and plagued the mental health professions, training and supervision must enter the age of client enlightenment" (p. 176). What in the world would the age of client enlightenment look like? First, it would look like professionals have begun to take the consumer of mental health services seriously. The key variables in effective psychotherapy, in terms of percentage of contribution to change, indicate that the major contributor to change is *the client*! Bohart and Tallman (2010) wrote an article in which they describe the client as "the neglected common factor in psychotherapy." How is that possible? If you accept that the client's active involvement is critical to success, then to what lengths are you prepared to go to maximize such an important variable? Bohart and Tallman (2010) suggest several implications for clinical training and supervision:

1. Therapists should enlist and promote client strengths, resources, and personal agency.

2. Therapists should believe that clients are motivated and capable of proactive change.

3. Therapists should promote client involvement: Psychotherapy is a collaborative endeavor.

4. Therapists should listen to clients and privilege their experience and ideas.

In short, are you willing to prepare yourself to engage in a working partnership with each and every client with whom you have the privilege to work?

Second, the age of client enlightenment means that the importance of the role of the client is meaningfully integrated into clinical training and supervision. It is essential to grasp what Bruce Wampold (2010) means when he says, "The logic is simple: It is the common factors...that lead to successful outcomes, and as long as those common factors are capably used by therapist and client, the treatment will be beneficial" (p. 56). Why? Because the common factors begin with the unarguable importance of all the things the client brings to therapy to help make it successful. How do we integrate something so important into all graduate education for future mental health professionals?

Here are some suggestions.

1. Take responsibility for the importance of your role as a therapist. One of the truly true truths in this regard is the fact that "much of the variability in outcomes in therapy is due to the therapist" (Duncan, Miller, Wampold, & Hubble, 2010). Allow your supervision to shape and mold you into someone who can help the client maximize her or his potential for change.

2. Take responsibility for creating the kind of relationship with your supervisor that you want to have with clients. Another variable clearly supported by common factors research is the importance of a positive alliance with the client. If the therapeutic relationship is the cornerstone of effective psychotherapy, begin as soon as possible in learning to develop that kind of relationship with your supervisor, who will be watching and hoping that you will be passionate about that kind of learning. Let's be honest: we are all a little blind to some of our own behavior. Be radically open about getting as much feedback as you can get your hands on about the way you create a therapeutic alliance.

THE HEROIC CLIENT-AS-SUPERVISOR?

If the client is actually directing the show in supervision, what is the role of the student? What is the role of the supervisor? In short, the goal of supervision is to make the client as real as possible in the deliberations of the student about how to help the client. No matter how much therapists talk about theory or research or insurance, not much happens in therapy without the client! Successful supervision enhances the student's ability to hear the client on the client's terms without qualification or minimizing. Here are some suggestions for learning to include the client's voice in your supervision:

- Audio and video tapes of a session
- Audio or video tape supervision to be shared with the client
- Include the client in your supervision
- Ask the supervisor to sit in on a session

- Role-play that allows the student or the supervisor to be the client

- Bring questions from the client to supervision

Every one of these strategies has been used by students and supervisors over the years. There are probably many others that you might imagine as you develop your clinical imagination. The point is to learn to be guided by the client's goals and preferences.

SALLY AND GREG TRY SOMETHING REALLY CRAZY

At one point in their training, Sally and Greg worked on the same practicum team even though they were in different years in their training program. They had been assigned a new client with whom they worked together, usually with a team, but often with only a supervisor watching them work from behind a one-way mirror. Not only was the client from a different culture than either Greg or Sally, but he also grew up in another country in circumstances hardly believable in terms of the kinds of families known to Sally and Greg.

The client attempted to explain the importance of his background for understanding his current situation. Unfortunately, Greg and Sally, not grasping the substantial cultural differences, pushed ahead assuming they understood what the client was trying to convey. At the end of the second session, the students asked the client to complete a quick evaluation to tell them how they were doing as therapists. To their surprise, the client evaluated them poorly. Shocked, Sally and Greg felt the air going out of their clinical balloons. Rapidly coming back to earth, they excused themselves to talk to their supervisor.

Confused and more than a little embarrassed, Sally was the first to say, "What are we doing wrong? I don't get it." Greg added, "This is a little scary. What are we missing? The client's presenting problem seems pretty straight-forward to me, but now I'm not so sure." The supervisor comforted them with reassurances that they made a wise decision to take a break from the session to check their own assumptions against the observations and experience of the supervisor. "This kind of thing can be confusing even to me," the supervisor admitted. "If you know you're missing something, but aren't sure what it is or how to correct the problem, you might want to slow things down to make sure you're hearing everything you need to be hearing."

"Why don't we ask the client what we're missing?" Sally asked. "For that matter," Greg suggested, "why don't we all talk to the client about it?" The supervisor smiled, knowing they were experimenting with some of the nonhierarchical approaches to working with clients discussed in recent course reading. "Let's do it," he said.

Back in the room with the client, Sally thanked him for allowing them to consult with their supervisor. She then explained that they would like to try something crazy and bring the supervisor into the room with them to enhance their ability to understand the client's story in a way that made sense to the client. The client agreed with the idea, not knowing what to expect, but appreciative of the students' efforts. After entering the room, the supervisor also thanked the client for being patient with the training process, but assured him that the point of all the going back and forth was to find a way to be helpful to him. The client smiled and thanked the students and the supervisor. "What do you think we are missing as we attempt to understand you?" Greg asked. Taking a deep breath, the client explained that his experience was so far outside the norm that he could tell the students were glossing over the importance of what he was trying to explain.

As the client went into more detail, the helpers had their dials set to "Really Serious Listening." They were shocked to see how their assumptions had deafened them to the client's story. Gradually they began to absorb what the client was actually trying to convey. The more they understood, the more emotional the client became about recalling the details of his experience. At the end, as he wiped tears from his eyes, he thanked them for going to the extra trouble of bringing the supervisor into their conversation. His voice quivering, he said "Nobody has ever gone to so much trouble to listen to what I went through." It was a lesson Greg and Sally would never forget.

CONCLUSION

For years I have said to students that the client will tell you everything you need to know—if you are humble enough to hear it. The authors of *The Heroic Client* suggest that "we push the inclusion of the client's voice further and encourage the client to act as a 'super supervisor'" (Duncan & Miller, 2000, p. 184). Don't be afraid to try something crazy if you think it might help you hear the client more accurately. In a sense, when you are in supervision, you are representing the client in whose interests you are eagerly searching every angle to be helpful.

The whole point of supervision ought to be how to include the client in the therapy process in a way that allows the client to engage therapy as an active participant. Maintaining a collaborative intention in therapy allows the therapist to align himself or herself with as much of the potential for transformation as possible. The client brings almost half of everything required for change to the therapy without the therapist doing anything! Who wouldn't want to make the most of that kind of motivation?

From the beginning, make a conscious decision to engage your supervisor with the intention to learn as much as possible about how to successfully engage clients. However you manage to do it, learn to take the risk of opening yourself to as much feedback as you can handle. In a sense, you are there representing the client. As in most sports, mastering the fundamentals is everything in successful psychotherapy.

So when the client asks, "Who's your daddy (or mommy)?" you know what to say, right? There will be many reminders as you proceed through your training process about how to creatively and consistently include the client in the therapy process. As you experiment with the various ways to include the heroic client-as-supervisor in your supervision conversations, remember that you are connecting the *why?* and the *for whom?* in your basic reasons for doing any of this.

CHAPTER 6 — DISCUSSION QUESTIONS

1. What is a better way of thinking about the client that is recommended in this chapter?

2. What are some creative ways you might include the client in your supervision?

3. If you were Sandy or Greg, how would you be feeling in the session discussed above?

CHAPTER 7

COMPETENCE: THE HOLY GRAIL IN SUCCESSFUL SUPERVISION

I F YOU LIKED THE ADVENTURES of Indiana Jones as he searched for the Holy Grail in the movie *Raiders of the Lost Ark*, you will love the newest adventures awaiting those preparing to become the next generation of mental health professionals. The Holy Grail in the context of instruction and supervision is *competency*. A competency is a professional skill that can be measured and verified. Academics and practitioners have identified several different kinds of competencies for which future mental health professionals will be responsible.

Professional counselors, psychologists, marriage and family therapists, social workers, chemical dependency counselors, and case managers will increasingly be expected to be able to show how and why what they are doing is effective in helping people. The public has every right to wonder if what we have been doing actually helps people. Even though research continues to support the conclusion that psychotherapy is unusually effective, the more aware consumers become, the more they will also have questions about what we do and why. Where the public has greater knowledge and awareness about what we do, we must be prepared to take on the extra burden of accountability to prove worthy of their trust. It is in our best interest to encourage the public's curiosity about what we do as professional helpers by showing the effectiveness of our work.

One way to respond to the need for increasing accountability is to focus more specifically and more explicitly on what mental health professionals will be doing well in their attempts to help clients. If we know how to do something well, we have established a *competency*, a measureable skill or behavior that makes the helping endeavor successful. In this chapter I will introduce you to a new way of thinking about how to measure success in the delivery of psychotherapeutic services. You will learn about core competencies and how they can show you from the beginning of your training the kinds of expertise that will be expected of you when you are able to practice on your own.

You still get to be you and practice in your own way, but the core competencies give you a chance to imagine some of what is expected of fully licensed mental health professionals. In this chapter, you will also hear about competency-based supervision and the important role it plays in preparing you for the kind of competence that will allow you to help the people in the "for whom" that we talked about in the previous chapter.

IDENTIFYING THE HOLY GRAIL

In 2002, the American Association for Marriage and Family Therapy (AAMFT) took the bold step of creating the Core Competency Task Force. The association gave the committee the task of identifying domains of knowledge and the kinds of skills that define the competent practice of marriage and family therapy. Two years later the task force identified 128 clearly defined competencies that would equip any therapist to be able to function independently and, of course, competently. The 128 competencies fall under six (6) domains or categories. They are as follows:

1. *Admission to Treatment:* Getting therapy started

2. *Clinical Assessment and Diagnosis:* Assessing individual and family functioning

3. *Treatment Planning and Case Management:* Developing a plan of care and coordinating care with other professionals

4. *Therapeutic interventions:* Effecting change in the therapy session

5. *Legal Issues, Ethics, and Standards:* Understanding the legal and ethical aspects of practice

6. *Research and Program Evaluation:* Knowing the relevant research and how to evaluate one's effectiveness

You will find all 128 core competencies on the AAMFT website.

Each of the six domains is broken down into five subdomains that further define the various levels of expertise.

1. *Conceptual:* Factual knowledge, i.e. the academic content in books, etc.

2. *Perceptual:* Ability to perceive or see what is going on with clients and in the therapy process

3. *Executive:* Skills and actions that enable one to execute or operationalize knowledge

4. *Evaluative:* Ability to assess one's abilities and performance accurately

5. *Professional:* Ability to adhere to professional and ethical standards

If all of this sounds like gobbledygook right now, you will become more and more familiar with it as time goes by. You will, I promise, become appreciative of the detail and specificity of the core competencies as you evolve as a mental health professional.

For many of us trained and nurtured in the family therapy movement, our first exposure to all of this was in the July/August 2005 issue of *Family Therapy Magazine*, published by AAMFT, which focused entirely on "Competence in Family Therapy." I remember feeling almost shocked by the possible implications for training programs. But I was also struck by how much more helpful it would have been to go through a program oriented to what I was learning to call "core competencies." In her article in the magazine, Dr. Thorana Nelson (2005) put into words what I was thinking and feeling when she wrote, "From early in my career, I have been frustrated that so much of what we call education focuses on what we want to teach rather than what trainees need to learn." Did you catch that? What matters when you are out there on the front line as a counselor or psychotherapist is not what Dr. Oh-So-Wise said about some obscure research he or she thought would change the world if only the rest of us could understand it, but rather *what we need to learn* to help the clients talking to us right now.

A NEW APPROACH TO TEACHING AND LEARNING?

Gehart (2010) calls the new educational paradigm a "learning-centered pedagogy" for a reason. Pedagogy refers to the art and science of education, the aims of which are finding ways to help learners with knowledge and skills acquisition. "In the years to come, the education and training of family therapists will increasingly employ learning-centered activities to enable students to more quickly learn the competencies required in today's practice environment" (Gehart, p. 5). Learning-centered means practical, useful, relevant, and confidence-inspiring. Such methods allow the student to integrate academic knowledge and clinical skills more quickly than the traditional content-oriented methods. Some of us still carry some resentment about our earlier training experiences because of such faculty attitudes.

In the future, we will be focusing on helping students learn competency skills by any means possible. If it helps to read a book, then read a book. If it helps to watch the instructor or more experienced students model a technique, then role-play is perfect. If you need to visit someone's private practice to see how it's done in the real world, plan a field trip! Watch movies. Talk to more experienced colleagues. Volunteer to participate in any learning opportunity you can find. This is the essence of good old pragmatism: Whatever works.

Is this different from what has been done in the past? Absolutely. Will it be easy? Probably not. Diamonds take time, right? There will be challenges for both faculty and students. "Learning-centered education may not be as safe and comfortable as traditional pedagogy, but it certainly is more exciting, more thorough, and more likely to get you out of your seat and moving" (Gehart, p. 5). In my experience in a radically collaborative training program, Gehart is exactly right. In my classes, we didn't sit down for very long. My classroom philosophy tells me that if we are moving, talking, and laughing, then we are probably learning.

What are some of the major implications for students? See if you find yourself recalling what I wrote about collaborative learning. Learning-centered means (Gehart, p. 5-6):

1. Learning is more than academic knowledge.

2. Learning is active.

3. Students apply ideas to real situations, learn to complete clinical forms, and learn to develop treatment strategies for actual cases.

Maybe you can begin to see the importance of being an actively and assertively engaged student who joins the supervisory conversation with confidence and anticipation. If you are open and respectful of your co-learners, including supervisors, you will contribute to a climate of collaborative learning that enriches everyone.

In addition, there is a steep learning curve for instructors. It is no longer enough to provide comprehensive content. Emphasis on core competencies pushes faculty to help students understand how content relates to and informs clinical practice. And again Gehart (p. 5) is reassuring: "I believe faculty will find that learning-centered education is more fun than traditional pedagogical styles and, surprisingly, often requires less faculty time and energy while accelerating the learning process." While collaborative learning takes different forms than the old-fashioned shut-up-and-listen approach to education, it can be more intense and more effective, without necessarily requiring more work.

SANDY AND GREG GET THE INSIDE SCOOP ON COUPLE COUNSELING

When it came time for their practicum team to learn about working with couples, Greg and Sandy both had doubts about their readiness to work with two people at the same time. They read a lot about marriage counseling and conjoint therapy, but actually having to work with a couple in crisis takes their learning to another level. Experiential learning requires an experience, right? But what if you have never had the experience before and you feel obligated to already have some measure of competence to help them? It can be a little anxiety-provoking to say the least. And that would be normal. If you allow the anxiety to persuade you to avoid the risk of the experience, you cannot learn from the experience. The trade-off requires you to find the courage to confront the anxiety and not allow it to control you. Working through your own anxiety is part of your learning how to help others do that same thing.

During one of the many long conversations with their practicum supervisor, Sandy and Greg puzzled about how to learn best about client expectations when it comes to working with a couple. More than once, their supervisor asked, "What do you need to learn?" It helped them to think about what they hoped to get from their learning. They watched several videos of master therapists working with couples. They even sat in with another team behind the one-way mirror to watch some more advanced students work with a couple.

While they were talking about the core competencies that relate to couple counseling, the supervisor was illustrating a point by talking about couples she had worked with over the past few months. Some had done well, others not so well. Sandy asked her, "Could we talk to one of them? Would it be possible to talk to one of the couples who had a positive experience in therapy about what it was like for them?" The supervisor thought it was a clever idea and told them he would think about how to bring it up with one of the couples she had seen.

Two weeks later, Sandy and Greg were sitting with their supervisor interviewing one of the couples about their experience in therapy. They were quick to thank the couple and to clarify that they only wanted to learn from their experience. The couple found the conversation to be reinforcing of what they had gained from therapy a few months earlier. It turned out to be a win-win for everybody. The students asked good basic questions about what the therapist did that worked and what did not work. As they talked, the students began to hear some basic themes about careful listening, including some tips about how to facilitate a conversation that allows all parties a chance to both speak and hear. Greg was struck by how much of what the therapist did was to slow down the conversation long enough for the couple to work on things they had not talked about before. Sandy had an epiphany of her own about how constructive a dialogue could be when it was both carefully and respectfully directed toward the goal of constantly evolving understanding. She noticed that when the therapists engaged them with that kind of attitude, the couple began to experiment with the same behavior which, in turn, helped them slow down enough to hear each other.

After the couple had gone, the supervisor pointed out to Sandy and Greg that they could no longer say they had never worked with a couple. Detecting confusion, she added, "The very best couple therapy is not much different from what you just did. What makes couple work effective has everything to do with the basic foundation you created together in the shaping of the kind of conversation you had with them." Both students realized what the supervisor was teaching them about experiential learning, and both now felt not only more *competent* but also more *confident* in their ability to work with a couple in therapy. Reviewing the core competencies relevant to working with couples, both were surprised to see how many they had experienced in the interview with the couple.

SUPERVISION WITH THE HOLY GRAIL IN MIND

If the Holy Grail of training as a mental health professional is *competence* or *competency*, you will not be surprised to hear that there is such a thing as a competency-based approach to supervision (Falender and Shafranske, 2004, 2012). If it is true that "supervision is the major means of transmission of the foundations of the psychology profession to students, trainees, and supervisees in development" (Falender and Shafranske, 2012, p. vii), then we need to be clear about what those foundations are and how to transmit them to students in a way that not only makes sense, but also contributes to their overall development as clinicians. I predict that you will hear a lot about competency-based supervision in the future.

I am reminded of what the late Stephen Covey (1989) wrote in his book, *The Seven Habits of Highly Effective People*. After Habit One, which encourages us to be proactive, Habit Two is to "Begin with the end in mind." As you begin your journey toward becoming a fully-functioning mental health professional, the core competencies will help you imagine your destination while learning to design your own maps for the journey.

CONCLUSION

Relatively new to mental health profession, core competencies allow us to find meaningful ways to be accountable to a public that is increasingly curious about what we do and why we do it. *Competence* is more than a word. It represents a holistic vision for the training and supervision of future helping professionals. Aspiring to develop a *competency* in one of the basic areas of expertise required for the effective delivery of mental health services means one will have mastered a skill that can be observed, measured, and evaluated by both therapists and clients.

The core competencies now guiding practice and training in multiple behavioral health disciplines are not meant to be shackles! If you find an instructor or supervisor who wants to tell you that there is only one way to perform a particular competency, head for the exit. The core competencies are designed to make us increasingly effective, rather than support an instructor's arbitrary control over you. You still get to be yourself as you evolve and develop in your own unique way. But make no mistake—the core competencies are here to stay, and as they are integrated more and more into learning-centered approaches to instruction, they will ensure that you will rapidly develop a high level of skill as a mental health professional.

CHAPTER 7 — DISCUSSION QUESTIONS

1. What is the Holy Grail of supervision, according to this chapter?

2. How do you plan to make use of the core competencies to enhance your professional development?

3. How do you feel about what Greg and Sandy did to learn about couple therapy?

CHAPTER 8
CONCLUSION: LESSONS FROM GRADUATION DAY

REG AND SANDY WOULD LIKE to thank you for taking the time to wade through this brief orientation to clinical supervision. They have already graduated from their training program and become effective and competent mental health professionals. You are not far behind them. They would tell you, "If we can do it, you can do it." They might also say that the struggle to integrate all the various levels of experience into a workable synthesis was worth the effort. Sandy would say, "Now I can see that there is no way around the anxiety that seems to be present the whole time I was in the program." I can hear Greg say, "I have a whole new appreciation for the role my supervisors played in my ability to get through all the confusion of the developmental process." Both will likely have tears in their eyes if they talked about how important their relationships with other students have become as they have grown together.

In the introduction I suggested that you will not be alone if and when you begin a training program toward the goal of being a mental health professional. It is possible that the vision I shared with you may be more challenging than I have imagined, but I remain convinced that things are changing in most training programs. I believe that you will be joining a rapidly growing community of people from all walks of life who see the tremendous need for competent, highly skilled professional helpers in today's society. Fortunately, you will be accompanied in the training process by experienced professionals who will supervise the developing work of future colleagues like you. They are the real student's guide to supervision. Not this book.

We have taken a whirlwind tour through what makes for successful supervision. We looked at the word "supervision" and an in-depth definition of the process entailed in that word. I suggested that it is a context, a relationship, a conversation, a process, a set of goals, and a set of standards for competence. It is the *sine qua non* of the training process. The Latin phrase means "that without which." The thing that makes everything work is the supervisory relationship. I also told you the truth about how normal it is to feel anxious and even overwhelmed from time to time. That normal nervousness does not have to control you, and it must not define you. You will work through it and get to a surprising level of calm self-confidence.

We discussed your role in successful supervision in terms of understanding your potential and the need to connect your potential with the transformative energy of a training program. Take ownership of your training. Take as much responsibility for your learning as you can manage. Your dream of being able to help people as a mental health professional is within your reach.

Be patient as you navigate your way through the normal and predictable developmental stages of professional growth. Remember that your attitude toward both personal learning and shared learning either opens or closes the horizons of your potential.

We then moved to the other side of the supervisory relationship: the supervisor. It may take you years to fully appreciate all the different kinds of responsibility your more experienced colleagues take on for your sake. Begin as soon as possible to engage your supervisor in an evolving dialogical relationship that will benefit both of you. I suggested that it might help you to appreciate the kinds of responsibilities supervisors cope with to consider all the various hats they must wear in order to be helpful to you. It can be a little nerve-wracking on both sides. You will need to learn to bear and share your part in the ethical responsibility borne by the whole family of mental health professionals for your training. It all begins with your relationship with your supervisor.

Next we explored one of the more recent developments in professional training: the role of the collaborative learning community in your supervision. There is no question that collaborative learning is more effective than learning in isolation. Remember: you are not alone, nor should you be. On one level, the whole point of your training is to fine-tune your ability to work with other human beings. You will learn a lot about yourself. Be radically open to seeing yourself as honestly and compassionately as possible. It will help you be able to do the same for your clients someday. I predict that you will hear more about the collaborative learning community as an ideal environment for training mental health professionals. Supervision takes place all the time on multiple levels in a collaborative learning community.

Last but not least, the role of the client in successful supervision begins to take on new meaning when you consider how much clients contribute to their own change. We would do well to think of them as heroic clients as I mentioned in the chapter. Everything that happens in supervision is on behalf of the clients you are attempting to help. You can experiment with the many different ways to include the heroic client-as-supervisor in your supervision. Keep the client in mind as you make your way through your program. It is likely that the way you engage your training is the way you will engage clients after you leave the program.

Competence and the revolution it represents will guide a more learning-centered impetus in training programs. There is a difference between what faculty members talk about sometimes and what you will need to learn in order to be helpful to future clients. Stay focused on what you need to learn. The core competencies will give you a complete look at what you will need to be able to do to practice independently. You cannot do better than begin with the books by Gehart (2010, 2014) and Falender & Shafranske (2004, 2012) to see the new direction of training programs.

I began with the promise that you will not be alone as you make your way to your dream of being able to work with people as a professional helping person. I am able to keep that promise only with your help. I keep that promise by encouraging you to find out about supervision from the earliest possible moment in your training and to be assertively and proactively engaged in all aspects of your professional development. You will invest in relationships with supervisors and with other students as much as you will invest in reading books and journal articles.

You will feel less and less alone as you feel more and more engaged with all the things that contribute to the development of your professional identity. You will learn a lot about yourself. Embrace that fact. The more humbly and honestly we can see ourselves, the more humbly and honestly we can be present with the hurting people who hope we can help them. You will also learn a lot about other people who may be different from you. That does not make them wrong. Again, the more humbly and honestly you can learn to collaborate with them in their development, the more humble and honest you will be with everyone you try to help.

There is a kind of romantic hopefulness in all of this that is more poetry than prose. Some of us are called to be "rivers" for other people. In Emeli Sande's song "River," she promises:

Wherever you're standing, I will be by your side
Through the good, through the bad, I'll never be hard to find.

Not a bad way to end. Keep up the good work and all of this will make a lot more sense as you get a little further down the road.

CHAPTER 8 — DISCUSSION QUESTIONS

1. What are some of your impressions of the messages in this book for readers considering becoming mental health professionals?

2. What else might you have wanted to see discussed in this book?

3. How successful has this book been in encouraging you to consider becoming a mental health professional or to more vigorously pursue the training program in which you are enrolled?

REFERENCES AND RESOURCES

AAMFT (2004). Core Competencies. *www.aamft.org/imis15/ Documents/MFT_Core_Competencie.pdf*,

AAMFT. (2005). Are you competent to practice marriage and family therapy? *Family therapy magazine, 4* (July/August).

Anderson, H. (1997). *Conversation, language, and possibilities: A postmodern approach to therapy.* New York: BasicBooks.

Anderson, H. (1999). Collaborative learning communities. In S. McNamee & K. Gergen (Eds.), *Relational responsibility: Sources for sustainable dialogues* (pp. 65-70). Thousand Oaks, CA: Sage.

Anderson, H. (2000). Supervision as a collaborative learning community. AAMFT *Supervision Bulletin*. Fall: 7-10.

Anderson, H. (2007). The heart and soul of collaborative therapy: The philosophical stance—a "way of being" in relationship and conversation. In H. Anderson & D. Gehart (Eds.), *Collaborative therapy: Relationships and conversations that make a difference* (pp. 43- 59). New York: Routledge.

Anderson, H. (2012). Collaborative relationships and dialogic conversations: Ideas for a relationally responsive practice. *Family Process, 51,* 8-24.

Anderson, H. & Goolishian, H. (1992). The client is the expert: A not-knowing approach to therapy. In S. McNamee & K. Gergen (Eds.), *Therapy as social construction* (pp. 25-39). London: Sage.

Anderson, H. & Goolishian, H. (1990). Supervision as collaborative conversation: Questions and reflections. In H. Brandau (Ed.), *Von der supervision zur systemischen vision.* Salzburg: Otto Muller Verlag.

Anderson, H., & Swim, S. (1995). Supervision as collaborative conversation: Connecting the voices of supervisor and supervisee. *Journal of Systemic Therapies, 7,* 54-70.

Berger, P. & Luckmann, T. (1966). *The social construction of reality: A treatise in the sociology of knowledge.* New York: Doubleday.

Bernard, J. & Goodyear, R. (1992). *Fundamentals of clinical supervision.* Needham Heights, MA: Allyn and Bacon.

Bohart, A. & Talman, K. (2010). Clients: The neglected common factor in psychotherapy. In B. Duncan, S. Miller, B. Wampold, and D. Hubble (Eds.), *The heart and soul of change: Delivering what works* (2nd ed.). (pp. 83-111). Washington, D. C.: American Psychological Association.

Boyd, G. (2011). *It Takes a Community: A Study of Supervision in the Our Lady of the Lake University-Houston M.S. in Psychology Program.* Unpublished dissertation. Tilburg University: Tilburg, Netherlands.

Bruffee, K. (1999). *Collaborative learning: Higher education, interdependence, and the authority of knowledge* (2nd ed.). Baltimore: Johns Hopkins University Press.

Campbell, J. (2006). *Essentials of clinical supervision.* Hoboken, N. J.: Wiley and Sons.

Cottor, R., Asher, A., Levin, J. & Weiser, C. (2004). *Experiential exercises in social construction: A field book for creating change.* Chagrin Falls, OH: Taos Institute Publications.

Covey, S. (1989). *Seven habits of highly effective people: Powerful lessons in personal change.* New York: Free Press.

Dole, D., Silbert, J., Mann, A., & Whitney, D. (2008). *Positive family dynamics: Appreciative inquiry questions to bring the best in families.* Chagrin Falls, OH: Taos Institute Publications.

Duncan, B. & Miller, S. (2000). *The heroic client: Doing client-directed outcome-informed therapy.* San Francisco: Jossey-Bass.

Duncan, B., Miller, S., & Sparks, J. (2004). *The heroic client: A revolutionary way to improve effectiveness through client-directed outcome-informed therapy.* San Francisco: Jossey- Bass.

Duncan, B., Miller, S., Wampold, B. and Hubble, D. (Eds.) (2010). *The heart and soul of change: Delivering what works* (2nd ed.). Washington, D. C.: American Psychological Association.

Falender, C. & Shafranske, E. (2004). *Clinical supervision: A competency-based approach.* Washington, D.C.: American Psychological Association.

Falender, C. & Shafranske, E. (2012). *Getting the most out of clinical training and supervision: A guide for practicum students and interns.* Washington, DC: American Psychological Association.

Gehart, D. (2010). *Mastering competencies in family therapy: A practical approach to theories and clinical case documentation.* Pacific Grove, CA: Brooks/Cole Publishing Co.

Gehart, D. (2014). *Mastering competencies in family therapy: A practical approach to theories and clinical case documentation.* (2nd ed.). Pacific Grove, CA: Brooks/Cole Publishing Co.

Gergen, K. (1994). *Realities and relationships: Soundings in social construction.* Cambridge, Mass.: Harvard University Press.

Gergen, K. (1999). *An invitation to social construction.* London: Sage.

Gergen, K. (2005). *Therapeutic realities: Collaboration, oppression, and relational flow.* Chagrin Falls, OH: Taos Institute Publications.

Gergen, K. (2009). *Relational being: Beyond self and community.* Oxford: Oxford University Press.

Gergen, K. & Gergen, M. (2004). *Social construction: Entering the dialogue.* Chagrin Falls, OH: Taos Institute Publications.

Goodwin, D. K. (2005). *Team of rivals: The political genius of Abraham Lincoln.* New York: Simon and Schuster.

Hakansson, C. (2009). *Ordinary life therapy: Experiences from a collaborative systemic practice.* Chagrin Falls, OH: Taos Institute Publications.

Harre, R. (1983). *Personal Being: a Theory for Individual Psychology.* Oxford: Blackwell.

Herlihy, C. (2006). Ethical and legal issues in supervision. In J. Campbell, *Essentials of clinical supervision* (pp. 18-34). Hoboken, N. J.: Wiley and Sons.

Hersted, L. & Gergen, K. (2013). *Relational leading: Practices for dialogically based collaboration.* Chagrin Falls, OH: Taos Institute Publications.

Hess, A. (2008). Psychotherapy supervision: A conceptual review. In Hess, A., Hess, K. & Hess, T. (Eds.), *Psychotherapy supervision: Theory, research, and practice* (2nd ed.). (pp. 3-23). Hoboken, NJ: John Wiley & Sons.

Hess, A., Hess, K., & Hess, T. (Eds.) (2008), *Psychotherapy supervision: Theory, research, and practice* (2nd ed.). Hoboken, NJ: John Wiley & Sons.

Hess, A. & Hess, T. (2008). On being supervised. In Hess, A., Hess, K. A., & Hess, T. H. (Eds.), *Psychotherapy supervision: Theory, research, and practice* (2nd ed.). (pp. 55-69). Hoboken, NJ: John Wiley & Sons.

James, W. (1970). *Pragmatism and other essays.* New York: Washington Square Press.

Lerner, P. (2008). The dynamics of change and outcome in psychotherapy supervision: A note on professional identity. In A. Hess, K. Hess, & T. Hess (Eds.), *Psychotherapy supervision: Theory, research, and practice* (2nd ed.) (pp. 25-39). Hoboken, NJ: John Wiley & Sons.

Lock, A. & Strong, T. (2010). *Social constructionism: Sources and stirrings in theory and practice.* Cambridge: Cambridge University Press.

McNamee, S. (2007). Relational practices in education: Teaching as conversation. In H. Anderson & D. Gehart (Eds.), *Collaborative therapy: Relationships and conversations that make a difference* (pp. 313-335). New York: Routledge.

Mead, G. H. (1934). *Mind, self, and society.* Chicago: University of Chicago Press.

Menand, L. (1997). *Pragmatism: A reader.* New York: Vintage Books.

Menand, L. (2001). *The metaphysical club: A story of ideas in America.* New York: Farrar, Straus, and Giroux.

Nelson, T. (2005). Core competencies and MFT education. *Family Therapy Magazine, 4* (July/August): 20-23.

Penn, P. (2009). *Joined imaginations: Writing and language in therapy.* Chagrin Falls, OH: Taos Institute Publications.

Peters, J. & Armstrong, J. (1998). Collaborative learning: People laboring together to construct knowledge. *New Directions for Adult and Continuing Education, 79,* 75-85.

Pope, K. & Vasquez, M. (2007). *Ethics in psychotherapy and counseling: A practical guide* (3rd ed.). San Francisco: Jossey-Bass.

Pope, K. & Vasquez, M. (2010). *Ethics in psychotherapy and counseling: A practical guide* (4th ed.). Hoboken, N.J.: John Wiley and Sons.

Sampson, E. (2008). *Celebrating the other: A dialogic account of human nature.* Chagrin Falls, OH: Taos Institute Publications.

Shotter, J. (2008). *Conversational realities revisited: Life, language, body, and world.* Chagrin Falls, OH: Taos Institute Publications.

Smedslund, J. (2004). *Dialogues about a new psychology.* Chagrin Falls, OH: Taos Institute Publications.

Sperry, L. (2007). *The ethical and professional practice of counseling and psychotherapy.* Boston: Pearson.

Stewart, J. (2013). *U & me: Communicating in moments that matter.* Chagrin Falls, OH: Taos Institute Publications.

Stoltenberg, C. & Delworth, U. (1987). *Supervising counselors and therapists: A developmental approach.* San Francisco: Jossey Bass.

Wampold, B. (2010). The research evidence for common factors models: A historically situated perspective. In B. Duncan, S. Miller, B. Wampold, and D. Hubble (Eds.), *The heart and soul of change: Delivering what works* (2nd ed.). (pp. 49-81). Washington, D. C.: American Psychological Association.

Watkins, C. (1997). *Handbook of Psychotherapy Supervision.* New York: John Wiley & Sons.

CPSIA information can be obtained
at www.ICGtesting.com
Printed in the USA
LVHW090018130122
708470LV00005B/163

9 781938 552229